Basic
Groupwork

Basic
Groupwork

TOM DOUGLAS

INTERNATIONAL UNIVERSITIES PRESS, INC.
New York

To Shirley

for all her help and support

Printed in the United States of America

Contents

Acknowledgement

I acknowledge my great indebtedness to those students, ex-students, colleagues, and friends who have willingly allowed me to quote from their precious records of group meetings, knowing how scarce good material of this kind is, but believing that to share it with others is one way of increasing expertise and consequently the amount and quality of groupwork in the future.

Preface

Interest in the use of groups has grown enormously over the last twenty years. I have worked with groups since 1953 in all kinds of different settings and have attempted to put my experience on record for others to use as they will.

However, one thing has become clearer the longer I have worked with and taught about groups, and that is how difficult it is to learn to work with them effectively. Why should this be so? I think there are several possible reasons. The first is the common concentration there has been on attempting to understand the individual, despite the obvious fact that we are born into a group and that groups of all sorts affect every moment of our lives from then on.

This concentration on the individual and his behaviour has left us with very few inclinations or abilities to respond to the crying need to understand the ways in which the groups, of which we are a part, have such an important influence on our lives. Far from enhancing our ability to choose what we will do by ensuring our individuality this lack of knowledge about group pressures of all kinds dictates that our choices are restricted and we are unaware of the fact. So much for the vaunted individual freedom! This fact is occasionally recognized when people in authority tend to excuse the behaviour of some lesser mortal by saying he was led astray. In other words, he succumbed to pressures to conform to some kind of life style — pressures of which he may have been dimly aware — or more likely he was under the impression that he had chosen what he wanted to do.

The second factor is cultural. Children are brought up in western society to consider themselves as unique individuals and to be largely unaware of their relationship to other significant members of their milieu. Thus most of us are insufficiently curious about others. We tend to accept that each has his own right to exist as he chooses and only at certain times on certain occasions are we prepared, under well signposted rules, to behave gregariously. But woe betide anyone who carries this sort of behaviour into those areas of our lives where it is deemed inappropriate. Imagine the furore such a character would cause in a commuter train on the way to work! Social distance and propriety ensure that we feel that we are in control of our lives and that others impinge only in well understood ways and when allowed to do so.

Traditionally we have always worked with individuals when they have been in need of help, except perhaps in education where, until very recently, the class could be seen as a collection of people, but was seldom treated as a group, i.e. as a functioning unit. In social work, again until fairly recently, the method of choice was an individual approach. Of course cognizance was taken of the fact that individuals existed in an environment among other people, which for better or worse actually had some effect on them. But in many cases this recognition was something of an afterthought.

In a sense then, having ignored groups as a medium for working with people for centuries, we approach them with all the bias that an individualistic outlook can produce. This book is a personal statement about my belief that groups of people can become effective entities in their own right, and that the behaviour of such entities is more predictable and thus more readily directed towards the ends that the group hopes to achieve than anything that can be done working with the separate individuals that comprise it.

This is in no way meant to imply the existence of a 'group mind' or to postulate that groups can think. Groups are always and ever composed of individuals. But conditions within a group which has 'formed' are such that the influence of the group on its individual members and the influence of the members on the group render possible significantly different behaviour on the part of the members than could have been expected had they been operating with only their usual and little understood ordinary pressures applying.

This factor and this alone makes it necessary to postulate that when such a group exists, to ignore its influence-potential in favour of working with individual members is to throw away gratuitously the most effective tool there is for working with people either for learning purposes, therapeutic purposes, or any other.

Indeed before a collection of individuals has reached the 'formed' stage of a group (sometimes merely the operation of time will achieve this) the processes which will identify the formed group are already in operation and are being influenced in all kinds of unsystematic ways based on the past experience of successful or unsuccessful manoeuvres in similar situations by the individuals involved.

I have based what is written here on what I have found myself doing over the years in group situations and on the things that I find myself repeating over and over again to those who would work with groups. I have omitted most of the references which would make this an academic text in favour of being able to present directly and as forcefully as I can a basic approach to groups which is not only effective as a means of working with groups, but has a large spin-off in terms of understanding group pressures, to which we are all subjected all the time. This last fact is indeed a worthwhile aim in itself. Anything which enables us to make decisions which are based upon a fuller understanding of the pressures and the choices available must automatically ensure that we are operating as more effective and self-directing human beings.

Working with groups of people is not easy. It is not even very economic of scarce resources, though this is one of the main reasons given for the use of groups.

There is a great mystique abroad today about the use of groups in education, in social work, and in therapy. Whole new languages are erected about the processes involved, which make the uncommitted feel that there is a great deal more to learn than is actually the case. In fact if the matter is considered in cold blood, the language of groups should be the language of everyday life for the simple reason that most of us spend a great deal of our lives living, working, and playing in a group context.

The problem, as I see it, is not so much to learn about what goes on in a group, but to be able to do something about it for the benefit of the group members, which is an entirely different kettle of fish. Admittedly, to be able to understand what one sees is the first step to being able to do something about it. But our common experience of living in group situations will be of inestimable help if only it can be organized.

The purpose of this book is then to help people organize the experiences they already have in such fashion that they can begin to understand what goes on in group situations. No book can hope to teach anyone how to run a group efficiently; this needs supervised practice, but at least some attempt can be made to show what basic and essential skills are and how they might be applied.

This is a book to be used by people who are interested in working with people in small groups, or large ones for that matter, to help them to experience the thrill of getting it right and of seeing and feeling the benefit that others derive from a good group skilfully run.

Groups are not the prerogative of the professional helpers. They are to be seen as a means of support and help for anyone, whether that help be in co-operation in improving facilities or the sharing of resources of knowledge, skill, sympathy, or understanding. Groupwork is not therefore a skill which can be acquired only by professionals; it can and should be learned by ordinary people to sustain them, to give them pleasure and satisfaction and their rewards of sharing in chosen aspects of their daily lives.

1 In the beginning

'Where shall I begin, please your Majesty?' he asked. 'Begin at the beginning,' the King said, gravely 'and go on till you come to the end : then stop.' [1]

Strangely enough, and despite the king's advice, few people when discussing groups start at the beginning. There are several possible reasons for this. One may well be that groups are such an ordinary aspect of everyday life that it becomes easy, though terribly misleading, to assume that everyone is therefore well versed and indeed knowledgeable about the beginnings of groups. Another reason could be that what stems from the beginnings is so interesting that people become fascinated by the flower and do not care or even feel the need to know what the seed was like.

From my interest in the history of my family name I remember a phrase which seems to me to be singularly appropriate at this juncture. Robert Bain writing about the family of Douglas said:

---

1   Lewis Carroll, *Alice in Wonderland*, Ch. 11.

Men have seen the stream, but what eye ever beheld its source?[2]

I am not implying that no eyes have ever turned towards the beginnings of groups, but it does seem that many people who become involved in groups start well down the course of the stream. This means that they have to take on trust the most essential fact of using groups, i.e. that they work; that they are effective in achieving certain outcomes. It seems almost as if such people believe that it is sufficient to accept that ends are achieved and the answer to the question why is not often asked for.

But in the beginning there must have been some realization of the potential value of groups and of the way in which these values could be used. I appreciate that all introductory writing must appear to some people to be stating the obvious. But what is obvious to one person is by no means equally obvious to another who may have had no apparent reason for even starting to think about it. One of the basic misconceptions which besets human communication is exactly the unchecked assumption that the obvious appears so to all those involved.

In order to begin at the beginning it is necessary to understand some simple facts about the human condition and to state the apparently obvious about the way in which human beings attempt to maximize their satisfactions, whatever they may be, in any kind of situation.

There is of course one other problem in attempting to state facts about the beginnings of groups and that is that the overwhelming need to be selective produces a very simplistic version. However this is inevitable and it is better that there should be some basis to start from than none at all.

In any attempt to find out what most people are most frightened of happening to them, I am always struck by the fact that these fears can almost without exception be related to some form of fear of isolation. This can be expressed in a variety of ways, ranging from death itself to some situation in which the

2 Robert Bain, *The Clans and Tartans of Scotland* (London, Collins), p.112.

individual wants, but is unable, to make any kind of contact with any of his fellow human beings. There is here some vague appreciation of the fact which we all try to avoid, that we are in some very simple but very direct and essential way dependent upon others for our very existence. Indirectly we are saying that we know we exist because others respond to us.

This can be carried even further by saying that we are so enclosed within ourselves that we have no way of getting outside ourselves to see what we are like from the outside. We can however monitor the apparent effects that we have upon others and in this way we can begin to check what it feels like from inside with what it appears to be like from the outside. But then we are compelled to realize that the monitoring equipment is ours, and is thus likely to be subjectively biased. However when this fact is known, then some allowance can be made for the bias and a kind of agreed baseline can be set up. Most people today are somewhat more aware of the fact that they are dependent upon others for most of the essentials of their lives and it does not take much extension of this idea to encompass dependence upon others for confirmation of ourselves. This point need not therefore be laboured. But the connection between it and the power of the group needs to be made exactly clear. For in the understanding of the source of group power lies the difference between effective work with groups and non-effective work.

In order to interact with others the first essential is that others should be present. Now this is not as simple as it appears at first sight. The actual presence of others is not an ongoing necessity. If no real people exist at any given time with whom to relate, then the people of the imagination will do just as well — perhaps not as satisfyingly as real people for we would have to imagine their reactions to us rather than see them as pieces of behaviour which we could fairly easily recognize.

To put the whole matter into a nutshell would be to say that our need of other people is absolutely basic to our continued existence. Apart from knocking my head against a wall and being aware of the pain, apart from my memory of previous contact with others, how do I manage to affirm my existence?

3

The answer is of course simple ... I note that other people respond to my presence. Not only do they respond but they respond in a variety of ways according to how they perceive my behaviour as it affects them at any given time.

In order to get a response from others I have to get within distance, social distance that is, so that we can interact. What is more, I have to stay within that distance for long enough for the attitudes of others to get past the formal stage — long enough for them to get to know me. Obviously if my behaviour is such that the others do not want to have me around, then this process will not take place. This is the crux of the situation. The fundamental need of affirmation can only be met by a degree of acceptance of me as a person by those others who will confirm me as an existing being. In order to obtain that acceptance and thus get the continued contact which assures me that I exist, I am going to produce behaviour which is acceptable to these others.

There is little need to elaborate this point. It is a commonplace of life that we behave differently with different groups of people and that also we behave differently as isolated individuals than we do in any group. The well-behaved little boy who becomes a small hooligan when with his peer group is responding to the pressures which that group are able to exert upon him by virtue of his need to be accepted by the group. This kind of situation can be encapsulated in a simple statement as follows: *the greater the need an individual has of being accepted by a particular group, the greater the pressure that group can exert on that individual.* Of course there are exceptions and we must now go on to look at these.

The pressure which the family group can exert on a small child is very great, largely because of the helpless state of such a child. Put another way, his needs are so great of that particular group that the group's ability to exert pressure is almost unlimited. However if the pressure so exerted is of a harmful kind, then the state steps in and attempts to adjust the situation more favourably to the child. Which brings us to the first of the exceptions mentioned earlier.

The great pressure which a group can exert upon an individual member is dependent upon there being no viable or even known alternative. Obviously if alternatives exist however less satisfactory than the original group they may have been to start with, they can soon become preferable if the pressure exerted by the chosen group becomes too great. This point becomes very important when we come to consider later the predicament of those group members who have no alternatives of any kind, perhaps they have been deliberately removed, and are yet subjected to great pressures. There are those also who are not aware of possible alternatives and who therefore feel that they have no choice but to submit to the pressures which are involved in their current situation.

It is possible now to state that one of the main sources of power which resides in a group is the need to be accepted and liked by other people. Without doubt the more that we respect, like or love or need the people who comprise the group the greater the amount of pressure we are prepared to sustain in order to gain acceptance. It is not without some very basic understanding of human nature that the major form of punishment for human beings has always been some form of enforced isolation. That people frequently choose isolation is no argument to the contrary. The choice is deliberate and in most cases can be rescinded at any given moment. In any case such seekers after isolation are quite able to sustain themselves on remembered contacts and upon imaginary interactions for varied lengths of time.

Other sources of the power of the group have to be considered here as well. Perhaps the most important of these is the factor of 'contagion'. All of us have on many occasions experienced the effect of being swept along by a group of people who were already caught up in some strong feeling. The whole range of human emotions can supply this effect, though some are notoriously stronger than others, for example, fear. People who have assisted in the commission of very serious acts when under the influence of group contagion, e.g. lynching, are frequently horrified at their behaviour when the effect of the group

5

emotion has both worn off and is no longer available. They are swept along and involved beyond the point at which their individual behaviour patterns would have arrested them.

Of course such acts are undertaken when the emotional contagion is very powerful. Nevertheless such behaviour indicates the kind of influence which can be exerted within a group even when the emotions are not as strong.

Another sort of group power exists in confirmation of beliefs, attitudes, and ideas. Most of the groups which we join voluntarily offer us confirmation of our more cherished beliefs. This is not to say that there is no element of conflict, there is, but in the main we tend to associate with others who back us. The power here lies in the fact that this is a very rewarding experience. There is a great deal of satisfaction to be obtained in a situation in which one feels that one is agreed with and that one's path is not isolated but supported.

Satisfaction is a very important idea in the understanding of the power of the group. What actually constitutes satisfaction for a given individual is very hard to define. There are many instances of people who are receiving treatment at the hands of others which to most of us would seem to constitute a great dissatisfaction. But yet they remain in that situation. If there are possible alternatives which are not taken up, then we must assume that in some highly individualistic way there are hidden satisfactions for that person which outweigh the alternatives. The sheer output of energy necessary to change the situation may well be more of a dissatisfaction than staying put.

Quite obviously the contact that some people manage to achieve with others is so small that almost anything is better than nothing. Any kind of contact, however harsh or hurtful, at least performs the function of indicating to that individual that he exists by provoking a response in another. Being hurt is in many ways for many people preferable to being ignored. In view of what was said earlier about the basic need for affirmation this is in no way surprising, but it does reflect rather badly on the state of human relations.

All groups supply social contact of some sort. This may not be the essential purpose of the group, but in all groups it exists. People who are totally unsatisfactory for the basic purpose of the group may well continue to be members, if they do not interfere with the workings of the group too much, solely to take advantage of the contact with others that the group offers.

Most of this can be summed up by saying that *human beings tend to stay in situations which maximize their satisfactions. When there is an alternative, dissatisfaction can only reach the level at which the alternative becomes more attractive before the individual will opt out.*

It follows from what has been said here that group experience is not only one of the most powerful formative influences in our lives, but that it is also ubiquitous. Let us take the example of the family.

Everyone is born into a group situation. Admittedly some of us have to be content with the smallest possible group, i.e. of two persons, but most of us are more fortunate and find ourselves in a larger group. However the dyadic relationship of mother and child is sufficient in itself to create the eventual recognition of the part other people play in our lives and to set up all the basic learning about response patterns, love, dislike, acceptance, rejection etc.

A family is a peculiar kind of group for a whole series of reasons which will repay a brief restatement here. First no choice is offered or possible about membership, at least as far as the birth of new members is concerned. People who become members of a family by adoption, fostering, marriage, or other form of acceptance, have a different basis for their original membership than someone who is born into a family. Relationships in the latter instance have an ineradicable base in blood ties and the parent/child relationship.

Of course some people would admit to thinking at some time or other of their own family as a 'group' — but few have gone further and looked closely at the ways in which it functions as a group. Indeed when asked to do so, many find it not only a difficult but somewhat embarrassing task which has elements of disloyalty about it.

What makes the family a group, but a very special group? Well first of all there is the blood relationship which will exist in no other group in exactly the same way. Then the relationship of all members to others has many very obvious patterns, e.g. mother/father, son/daughter, and these roles have some heavy cultural significance which is not readily found in the roles created in other forms of groups. The family is a group which has the responsibility for socializing its younger members and of transmitting the culture in which it exists; for providing for its members in terms of their basic needs and of establishing their adjustment to society.

The authority structure has traditional and cultural elements and the relationships established last for the life of the members.

Comment has already been made about the dependent state of the child and thus the almost total power over him that the older members of the family can exercise. Of course each new member of the family learns fairly soon what effort produces satisfactory results and what does not. Indeed one might grossly oversimplify and say the baby must learn four things:

1 Not all needs will receive immediate gratification.
2 Some needs may not be met at all.
3 Some needs will be met by substitution.
4 Some needs will be met after different degrees of post-ponement.

In these areas of learning and the degree to which opportunity for learning is offered and taken up lies the basic socialization pattern of the infant. Certainly variations and complications exist, but the patterns of response learned in these areas tends to set the basic response patterns for life by generating the degree of ability to accept further learning along these lines.

This leads directly to a consideration fundamental to the business of working with groups. If it can be argued that our basic response systems are instituted and continually reinforced or affected in some way by group situations, then it would follow logically that if we need to:

(a) learn new and extra patterns,
(b) adjust some of the old ones to new and changed circumstances,
(c) increase the supportive nature of the ones we have, or
(d) re-learn some patterns which have proved to be maladaptive,

as some possible examples, then the same kind of organization as that in which the patterns were learnt in the first instance *should* form the best instrument to effect the change.

Some people would argue that this statement precludes the possibility of a rational and reasoned approach to change. Not at all, it merely implies that rational methods were only part of the original techniques of pattern-response-creation and cannot therefore, in any logical way, be presumed to be alone capable of achieving much change in them. In any case many patterns of behaviour are not to that extent under rational control, largely because their existence is unknown or has been forgotten, which comes to the same thing in the end, and their performance is habitual. Thus the first step in changing such patterns must be the generation of an awareness of their existence and of their consequences. I would hazard that, of necessity, this means some form of monitoring of the responses provoked in the presence of a number of people. By implication this would mean a group.

One very simple factor which is very important here is that of number. It is relatively easy to resist the response that we get from contact with one person, if we do not like it, by attributing it to bias of some kind. It is much more difficult to resist the same response from a number of people at the same time. The weight of numbers is taken as evidence of the existence of behaviour which carried a high degree of conviction.

The establishment of a group then has as its *raison d'être* the fact that the instrument has the same basic qualities as that which creates behaviour patterns. Nor is this just applicable to groups where the basic aim is therapeutic, reformatory, or to effect change; it also applies to groups where the enjoyment of leisure activities, social contact, or the dissemination of information is the main aim.

Let us look for a moment at the idea of the 'specialist'. Such a person has skills and knowledge in a particular area of human functioning which are generally regarded as being of a higher order than obtains in the ranks of the general public, i.e. the rest of us. If the skills and knowledge of the specialist are seen to be relevant to our situation, then if possible we make a bid for their use on our behalf. But there is an unfortunate limitation in this model which concerns the limits of professional knowledge and skill in certain areas of human experience. Thus if my TV set breaks down I would expect the skills necessary to repair it to be readily available — after all, TV sets were designed and built by human beings. Now when it comes to my mind or my body breaking down or even malfunctioning in some way, the expertise available to deal with the problem is not of the same order. Man did not create man in the sense of the TV set and his understanding of man-type problems is of necessity much more speculative and based upon cumulative experience. Of course the complexities of one situation and its possibilities are astronomically larger than the other.

So the specialist in human beings is at two disadvantages. First, his knowledge of the system is not that of its creator and second, while TV sets do not and cannot attempt to treat other TV sets, human beings treat other human beings. The point is that for a considerable range of human experiences the method of coping is empirically founded, each human being having to discover those effective for himself.

Such is the structure of our society that the coping behaviours one person discovers for himself are seldom passed on to other people. Herein lies one of the major advantages of a group, especially if it is composed of people whose experience of life is similar — they can each share with the others the ways they have discovered of coping. Not only does such a sharing carry a great deal of conviction and weight, it puts forward two major advantages. First, the recognition for each sharer that others have coped with similar problems and second, a great deal of faith in the validity of help from people who have themselves been through the fire becomes apparent.

The specialist's knowledge may be more extensive and his experience greater, but his understanding must in most cases be at least at one remove from the actual problem he is trying to cope with, apart from the ordinary problems of just 'being', that is.

Now in one sense everybody is a specialist, that is, we all possess knowledge and experience which is not commonly available to others. I refer of course to each individual's unique experience of life and his cumulative knowledge of the business of living. However poor his ability to cope may have been, at least he has experienced it and this experience may form the basis of the development of better coping behaviour in the future. How many times has advice, clearly, precisely, and accurately constructed failed to achieve change in someone's behaviour patterns? The reasons are often complex but are usually concerned with three areas of human interaction.

First, there may be no real desire to change. In order to change people have to see or believe that the change will enhance their satisfactions or bring rewards. Frequently there is no way of proving that increased satisfaction will ensue from pursuing a course of action other than taking the risk and setting the change in motion. Many people are bound by their inability to make this decision involving risk.

Second, there must be an underlying suspicion of people who offer help when it is clear that they themselves have only a theoretical knowledge, i.e. a non-personal experience, of what they are advising about. They cannot, as it were, know the problem from the inside. Of course this is not always either necessary or important, but there are many areas of human experience where it is.

Third, the credit of those who have had personal experience and survived, or, even better, enhanced their life style, is high. Here is demonstrable proof that it can be done, not by people with very different assets and life styles, but by ordinary people. Upon such an emotional commitment is based the success of Weight Watchers, of Alcoholics Anonymous, and of other groups, all of whom eschew the specialist but use common experience as a basis for change.

Now let us try and draw all these threads together. What we have been talking about latterly could be called 'shared experience'. It is not too strong a statement to make, that 'shared experience' is the one major factor which makes the difference between a number of people in a given place, a collection that is, and a group. The strength of a group lies in the recognition by its members that they have 'gone through' a lot together. This does not imply harmony or even agreement — it does imply the recognition of time spent in each other's company. If that time has increased the members' satisfaction, so much the better, so much the stronger the recognition of indebtedness to others.

So before any groups are created for specific ameliorative or other purposes, we are compelled to recognize that groups have had a monumental part to play in shaping the way we are, behaviour patterns, thought patterns, the lot. It is a bitter thought to many that our much-vaunted individuality and independence is at best the result of this conditioning process and may also come about as a reaction to it, if we have been made aware that it exists and of its effects. What we are trying to understand then is absolutely basic to human existence. Which leads to another point.

Given that group processes are so basic to our existence our acceptance of them must be a matter of habit. This would mean that many of the decisions we attribute to our individual assessment of situations are in reality mostly preconditioned responses over which we have little or no control. Some beginning understanding of group processes has two immediate and valuable spin-offs. First, some increase in the element of 'real' choice is almost inevitable because each of us can become at least more aware of the factors which are affecting our decision-making processes. Second, there is also the possibility of helping others to achieve some insight.

What follows is a verbatim report taken from a tape of a group of social work students which in many ways serves to highlight the discussion so far. The group had been together for some time when the recording was made, though there are many obvious signs that they have not developed a level of commitment to each other or to the group as a unit which would allow them to tackle the task unimpeded by relationship problems. The major aim of the group was to learn about the ways in which groups function and, with the help of a leader, to use their own group by analysing its stages and their relationship to it. Incidentally in the process of doing this there were some very obvious increments in personal growth, though the group was not primarily an instrument for increasing the members' sensitivity. The recording extract given here starts towards the end of one two-hour session.

Group leader   Thank you. I think it still boils down to the fact that we're being excessively cautious, and we're still not trusting people very much, even after last week's demonstration of the fact that if you do put yourself at risk, nobody sort of slays you. In fact people are most grateful for it.

     H.   In fact that's when the session's good, isn't it, when somebody does lay themselves on the line?

Group leader   Yes.

     H.   And if somebody was to do it now, no doubt we would produce the same thoughts as last week.

Group leader   I have a distinct feeling that you are asking someone to lay themselves on the line.

     H.   But that's when we feel the group is being successful!

Group leader   Yes. It becomes interesting doesn't it? You begin to realize that a lot of the things we've talked about in abstract, intellectually actually, can be appreciated through feeling. You can feel supported by people, you can feel that you're safe. One of the things I remember most clearly from last week — I'm sorry to keep harping back but it seems to be the only

13

thing that's sparking us at the moment — was the element of warmth that you generated — a sense of feeling towards people, and were warm and sympathetic and understanding. I think it's rather significant that Je chose this opportunity to bring up that bit about being closed off. Because I pointed out about the fact that we discussed this last term. At the risk of being repetitive, can I say one thing? Groups generate their energy from the amount that people put into them. There is no energy just floating about in space for you to pick up on. Groups are composed of individuals, and individuals have got the energy which they either put into it or withhold from the group situation. When people withhold energy from a group situation, the group tends to die, like not watering a plant. So you will find yourself quite frequently involved in a discussion with people in a group as to why they are withholding energy, and one of the major reasons is the one which we put forward here, and that is that we are rather frightened of the outcome, and it's pretty inhibiting when J. says, for instance, that he could talk all day, and yet he talks for about two or three minutes and then shuts up — why J.?

J.   Because I'll only say things that are of some relevance to the situation. I won't talk for the sake of it. I have to be motivated to talk, so I need something to talk about.

Group leader   Isn't the fact that the group might die on it's feet if you don't talk, a motivation?

J.   Well I was going to say something before but you put me off actually.

Group leader   Did I put you off? Alright...

J.   I was going to say to Je, because after the

session last week you were saying you doubted the validity, you couldn't see the use of some of the things that went on last week. I'm not putting you on a spot am I?

S. Are you kidding?

J. It struck me that when H. said that the group ran better when someone lays themselves on the line, is a bit unhealthy in a way ... a warning almost.

B. Yes.

Group leader Please sacrifice yourself ...!

B. Yes.

H. True.

Group leader But if that's good group work!!!

H. That's another issue I think.

B. Shouldn't it come out naturally, rather than people suddenly ... somebody saying well I'm going to do it now. I find it hard to know how to go about it really in those sort of terms, because I could see it coming out in a sort of spontaneous reaction to what other people say.

J. Yes.

B. Rather than a conscious effort.

N. I must say I'm a little bit puzzled, because after saying all about the warmth that was generated here last week, and this is the twelfth hour that we have been together as a group, I'm a little puzzled by everyone just sitting and not contributing.

Group leader What kind of feeling do you pick up?

N. It's difficult really because I'm trying to really come to terms with my own feelings about this, and in some way my own disappointment, I think, when you were talking about warmth that you generated last week, I think I wanted to share in it this morning, and you

15

know, I feel that it's either not here, or I'm not sharing in it.

S. Do you know what I think is wrong? I think that where I'm sitting is not so good, because I think that this break here ...

B. Yes. That's true.

S. I've just noticed that I've been hiding away from everybody else and opting out.

B. I like it better in a way because I like to see everybody, not like sitting on a bus. I think you've got to move ... can you see me? ... you can now?

Group leader Well the group is showing awareness of the need to do something about the situation.

J. Do you get a warm feeling if you contribute? Because I didn't feel particularly warm last week because I didn't say much. I find if I say something it's a much better group. The more I say the better it is ... seriously you know.

N. I suppose really I've never contributed so I've just never experienced it.

J. So you've never felt the warmth of the group?

N. I don't know that I've really thought very much about it. I haven't thought very much about my contribution to the group ... I think.

J. I don't have to consciously think if I've said it, I feel it, I don't know if anybody else feels this?

S. Well I felt it the opposite up to last week, when I said anything in the group session I kind of say my piece, and then sit back and think to myself was that alright? Did I say something good? I feel kind of embarrassed for about five minutes while I've worried it out and kind of had a rest.

C. I think I've felt like that on occasions but I end up analysing myself thinking that you made another wisecrack, sort of thing ... you know ... why did you do that? and would sit back holding my breath.

B. Then you go back into your own thoughts, what you said and how people appeared to have responded and you miss out the next five or ten minutes sometimes, if there is a next five or ten minutes.

Group leader I feel that's true. I think that probably because we are people who use our brains quite a fair bit, and when our relationships with people, particularly in a closed situation, things get a bit sticky, what you tend to do is go back into your own mind and we see ourselves as being gainfully occupied, if we're thinking.

B. Rather than saying to each other I'm not on the wavelength, I haven't really agreed with what you've said.

Group leader Instead of verbalizing exactly what one's thinking, by saying I feel that I'm now withdrawing from the situation because I can't get a response, sort of thing. If you do this kind of thing, do you think it's feasible that this is the kind of thing that a client group could do as well, and if so what are you going to do about it? Why did that stop everybody?

S. Because ...

Group leader Suddenly if you look round the room there are about two people whose eyes were ranged above floor level. You know you are using all the devices of the intelligent person to cut yourself off. You don't look at people, you look at the floor and things like that, I'm being a bit critical I must admit.

B. I thought, you know, that when my mind went off at a tangent I was thinking, what if

17

we had someone in the group who was very talkative ... we all said that we find M. very warm and I feel it strongly, I miss her when she's not here. But if we had someone who just wouldn't shut up ... which M. doesn't do ... M. is very sensitive to people's ... any messages we send out. But I was thinking of if we had someone who just wouldn't shut up, how would we react to that? Which is the exact opposite of us because we all turn in on ourselves. When you said a client group ... because I think clients are very different from us.

Group leader   This could be!

J.   Certainly as a group we obey the courtesies of group discussion. It is so courteous that nobody says much at all, to give other people a fair chance — well when we went off to the prison, a group of prisoners there ... we had about four groups going, they were all in one group but they were all talking to each other, the opposite sort of problem to this group.

B.   That's right.

J.   We've certainly played by the rules, but we're not just very playable.

Group leader   There is a whole series of rules in a group situation for protecting yourself and for protecting other people. Talking too much is just as much a protection in some circumstances. I think if you had one person in this group who talked too much, let's take it as a purely hypothetical situation, you would all sit back and think ah! I don't have to do anything maybe for quite long periods of time, because the pressure would be off.

S.   I don't know but I think the pressure would build up ...

This group could be called 'artificial' in the sense that it was created for an express purpose. But it demonstrates all the factors discussed earlier. Members are becoming aware of the responses they provoke from others and of the need to clarify their own responses. They are clearly becoming conscious of the way the group is developing, critical of themselves and of their fears, beginning to discover that commitment really means something beyond personal security and seeing that the whole group is the responsibility of each member.

Very interestingly the comments of the member who was absent from the previous session show very markedly her perception that the others had added to their shared experience and that she felt that she would like to have shared it also. Each member of the group is starting to help the others by stating what he sees, what he has learned; each is continually making points which help to clarify and consolidate the process of learning about group behaviour.

Such are the beginnings of groups and we must now turn to look at the many ways in which groups are manifested, created by human beings for beneficial purposes for themselves and others.

2 A very diverse family

Before any cautious person starts to use a machine or tool he tends, if he is wise, to find out what the main properties of the tool or machine are. A great deal has been written and said about the properties of groups and much time has been spent on trying to define them.

Groups are a little like dogs. Anyone who knows nothing about dogs must surely be puzzled by the diversity of creatures which apparently belong to the family of 'Dog'. To recognize that all these very different creatures have in fact arisen from the same basic stock is to recognize that they all have certain features in common, and the diversity arises from the fact that they have been bred for different purposes in the long history of the association of man and dog.

I am not claiming that the same degree of diversity exists with regard to groups as with dogs. But I do maintain that groupwork literature is very responsible for establishing the appearance of a multiplicity of groups which are all claimed to be something special and which hides the common ancestry.

> Ay, in the catalogue ye go for men.
> As hounds and greyhounds, mongrels, spaniels, curs
> Shoughs, water-rugs and demi-wolves are clept
> All by the name of dogs: the valu'd file
> Distinguishes the swift, the slow, the subtle
> The housekeeper, the hunter, every one
> According to the gift which bounteous Nature
> Hath in him clos'd; wherebye he does receive
> Particular addition, from the bill
> That writes them all alike; and so of men.[1]

In view of the acknowledged difficulty that exists in starting a group, it would be as well before we proceed any further to have a close look at this area. The first thing that has to be said about it is that the textbooks have treated it in a very chauvinistic way. By this I mean that if the text is directed at social workers, then the formation of social work groups is referred to; if it is directed at therapists, then the usual doctor/patient relationship kind of approach is discussed. There is seldom any recognition that other people than the audience at whom the book is directly aimed might be interested in running a group. Thus when we look for basic information about the ways in which groups are founded the material is strictly limited.

The origins of groups

At the risk of oversimplifying the problem I would state that there are five main ways in which groups are created. Perhaps it would be more accurate to say that there are five main situations from which groups may arise. They can be listed as follows:

1 The group is already in existence.
2 It just happened.
3 It came from public or partially public advertisement.

---

1 William Shakespeare, *Macbeth*, Act III scene i, ll. 92-101.

4 It arose from the splitting into sub-groups of a large public meeting, and

5 It was created by individual selection from a known public.

This list acknowledges the fact so often ignored by group workers that groups are not necessarily the closed, intense experience units which so often seem to be regarded as the norm. This is only one end of a fairly large continuum at the other end of which are large communities comprising many not too clearly defined smaller groups.

One other fact needs to be mentioned before we have a detailed look at these diverse origins of groups and see some examples of all five ways and this is the effect that the different kinds of start have on the groups which grow from there. It is not too simple to say that the way the group is created tends to dominate its life from start to finish and more than this it tends also to promote significantly different practice which is appropriate to the needs of the group.

None of these five categories of origin are totally mutually exclusive, but each category is clearly different from the others in certain very important characteristics.

1 *Already in existence* Examples of this are numerous and frequently this category of groups is referred to as 'natural' which simply serves to distinguish it from groups which are created especially for some beneficial purpose. Some of the main members of this category are the family, the gang, the work-group, the friendship group etc. The main identifying feature, as far as the group worker is concerned, is that the group was set up in the first instance for a purpose different from that which he may have in mind for it. Here lies the crucial factor, however the members of the group see themselves, the group worker sees them as members of a group and he works with them with this set in mind. Few families have ever thought of themselves as a 'group' exactly in that sense so the groupwork approach highlights dynamics which were hidden under the mantle of being a 'family'.

22

Graham suddenly began to talk about a drawing he had made on the blackboard and he brought it over to show me. It was of an African hut and there was a good deal of red in the picture, which seemed to be both fire and sun. This picture seemed to mean a great deal to him, and he drew it again and this time he said it was on fire because a car had crashed into it. He said, when I asked him, that he sometimes worried that their own house might catch fire. I commented on the way Graham was showing some of his feelings to us, and his parents were quite caught up and fascinated by this.

There was a lull in the interview, and Mr Roberts made an attempt to start a discussion about Martin's backwardness in school, and Martin responded with his bright, effortless chatter. I suggested that Graham and Martin might well think they were having to do all the talking, and I asked Martin what he thought of this? He became suddenly serious and pointed to his parents,

'Those two ought to talk.'

'What ought they to talk about, do you think?'

'They should talk about *their* worries.'

'Do *you* know what they are worried about?'

'They are both worried about work', desultorily playing as he spoke, then looking up and pointing: 'He's worried about some man at work — and she is worried about Wall's ice-cream!'

Incomprehensible to me but not to the parents! It then turned out that mother had taken a part-time job selling ice cream to try to pay off a pressing debt. She talked about her anxiety over the family's financial position with some difficulty, and her dislike of having to leave the boys with a neighbour. She didn't go into details but it seemed a relief for her to speak at all.

Mr Roberts then asked Martin what he thought he, father, worried about. Without giving the boy a chance to reply, he went on to say that he didn't generally worry about work, but there were one or two people he didn't get along with, but this was a very trivial problem. Whereupon Martin piped up and said, 'You are worried about that man you want to get rid of and no one else wants!'

Even Mr Roberts was stunned to silence by this. It was his present worry in a nutshell. Mrs Roberts said that although it had been mentioned, it had never been put in so many words in front of Martin. On this most cogent piece of family communication we ended this interview, all four quite committed to family group therapy.[2]

Here is a family seen as a therapeutic group by a social worker and beginning to see themselves in terms of group dynamics. Confronting roles are taken by those not normally used to such roles, and behaviour is being exposed in ways compatible with a 'group' but not normally associated with everyday family life.

2 *The group that just happened* This category is much like number one but instead of someone from outside coming to shove the group into seeing itself as a different kind of group, this is usually done by some member of the group. A pertinent example of this would be a group of business men who travel by the same train every morning and gradually build up a travelling relationship which they attempt to guard. During the course of conversation they become interested in the ideas of one of the group to start an amateur dramatics group. Eventually they form the nucleus of the society and use their relationship as a solid base.

There are many other possible examples of the way that a group seems to emerge spontaneously to meet an arising situation. Roles are accepted by people because they have a sense of the role being fitting both to the occasion and to themselves as people and are prepared to take the risks involved as they see them.

If we analyse further groups which appear to arise spontaneously without question, we are liable to discover that individuals had perceptions of the situation and made moves to

2   Ann Needham, 'Working with the family as a group', *Social Work Today*, vol.3, no.3, 4 May 1972, pp.2-6.

fulfil what they saw as necessary to meet that situation and in so doing were able to pull others with them. Where such moves did not result in others being drawn in and becoming active participants, then no group formed anyway. Perhaps the most important factor that the initiators of such a group need is an awareness that within the collection of people they are contemplating involving there exist the skills and abilities necessary to meet the bill, if they are used co-operatively.

3 *From public or partially public advertisement* When someone feels that he has something which may be of value to others whether it be an object or a service, then that person is liable to want to establish contact with those who could be interested in obtaining whatever he has to offer. Our society offers many services to others by the process of advertising, and group practitioners are not in any way averse to advertising that they believe their services will be of value to others. Professional journals contain many such advertisements, but local papers may also be the starting point for some ventures, as witness the extract given below from a report by a social worker of the establishing of a local 'Gingerbread Group'. It offers an example of both public advertising and also of a public meeting.

It was decided to organize a first meeting for anyone interested and then take it up from there if enough support was forthcoming. A suitable meeting place was needed, as it was felt that the group should not be seen as part of the Family Advice Centre, nor as an extension of the flats complex, but as an independent group for the town. A youth club in the centre was hired, and advertisements put in two local newspapers. Some financial support was given by the Social Services Department, and therefore initial payments were able to be met from these funds. Social workers in the area were asked to direct any single parents who might be interested in joining to the first meeting, which was held on Saturday 24 July at 10.30 a.m.
Refreshments were provided, which were paid for from

community development funds and prepared by two of the ladies interested in the group.

Invitations were sent out to approximately fifty people known to be single parents, and various mums' groups were informed and invited. Seventeen people attended the first meeting, and listened to a talk by the local organizer, who explained the purpose and aims of Gingerbread. There was a hard core interest in commencing a local club of about ten people, who agreed to meet the following Saturday to formalize proposals. After two or three meetings it was obvious that a group could be a going concern and despite numerous teething troubles the Gingerbread group did get off the ground, a committee was formed and a programme of events was issued. More suitable accommodation was needed as evening meetings were felt to be preferable to Saturday meetings, and also the youth club needed its rooms for themselves. It was decided that meetings would be held every first and third Thursday in rooms rented out to the Gingerbread group at a nominal fee by the Council for Voluntary Services.

Gingerbread now meets at fortnightly intervals, and the meetings are designed for friendship and discussion and members are able to give help and support to each other at times of stress and difficulty. Their calendar is full of social and fund-raising activities, a task which at best is difficult, but more so for a financially deprived group such as Gingerbread.

4 *From a public meeting* In one very essential sense a public meeting is a form of public advertising. The general public are invited to attend a meeting at which some problem or issue will be talked about, information will be offered and help with the problem requested. People attending such meetings may become interested and are invited to join groups whose purpose is to work to produce a solution to the main problem. It may be to visit old people, to provide cash for various ventures, to find accommodation for homeless people, to form working parts of an association with recreational, leisure, or educational ends etc.

Many national societies hold public meetings with the purpose of recruiting members to their local associations. Such recruits will thus join small groups which have tasks to perform. They may never need to establish a very strong cohesive spirit, but they do need to develop a level of co-operation compatible with the job they have to do. The drop-out rate is frequently high, apart from a stable nucleus which is responsible for the drive to recruit new members and which operates as in all open groups to perpetuate the group, to transmit its culture, and to ensure that its tasks are, as far as possible, achieved.

5 *Selection from a known public* When most people refer to groups created for an express purpose they are usually referring to groups which originate in this way. Basically an individual who is aware of the need of a definable section of the community decides that at least some of those needs can be met by bringing together some of that section into small groups. What is fundamental here is that the people comprising the section of the populace are already known and their situation is also known and the possibility of help being given through the medium of the formation of small groups is feasible. The range of possibilities is vast, from one-off groups which settle an issue there and then and do not need to meet again, to long term, social and therapy groups.

Populations are also defined in many ways, e.g. by location; residents' hostel, a hospital ward, a neighbourhood etc.; by handicap, the mentally ill, the physically handicapped, the disadvantaged, the delinquent etc.; by treatment, by need and so on — in fact all categories of people who need the services of others either long or short term.

Angela Simmons writing in *Community Care* about a group for Child Minders offers a good example of the way such a group is established.

To start with a list of 16 daily minders, mostly registered, was drawn up — all living within walking distance of the hall. Each of them was visited and the idea of a group discussed with them. 'Doubtfuls' were visited twice. A week before the starting date a letter went out to each minder inviting her to attend.[3]

Clearly the population was known and the problems of their occupation also known. The express aims of the group were listed as:

1 The minders should feel less isolated in their work.
2 They could share their problems about child minding.
3 They might increase their personal awareness and their insight regarding the children and their parents, and
4 They could exchange information and knowledge of resources.

The overall aim was of course to improve the service offered.

Many groups organized by the 'helping' professions fall into this category — in that the potential members are selected from a much larger group with whom the professional is already in contact.

This has led to a charge that such groups are artificial in the sense that families, work groups, friendship groups, and communities are not. The charge has no substance because no group is artificial in the sense that it is composed of 'real' people, the fact that their being together at one time in one place has been stage-managed adds nothing to a situation which is duplicated in 'real' life many times a day, but where the consciousness of the participants is not so clearly directed to the purpose of the group or its outcome.

Groups which have an existence prior to the arrival of a practitioner have the added complication of having been created for a purpose other than that which the practitioner eventually attempts to establish. The fact that such an alternative purpose can be established, and that such a group can be as successful as any other in achieving its purpose, indicates clearly that group processes exist in *any* group and that the ways in which they are directed make the differences in outcomes possible and give to *any* group a flexible range.

3 Angela Simmons, 'Helping minders help themselves ...', *Community Care*, vol.1, January 1975, pp.21-24.

As we shall see later most groups, whatever their kind or origin, have a great deal in common. Here we are concerned to show their differences.

Perhaps the simplest distinction of groups is into natural and created groups. The distinction is more apparent than real though it does become significant when a leader is imposed from without. Thus a natural group is one which arises from some situation in a spontaneous way. The most important of the natural groups has always been held to be the family, which grows from the natural bond of parents and the dependent state of children in their early years. Other natural groups are friendship groups and some forms of work groups. In essence these latter are groups which have arisen for reasons other than the creation of the group itself.

A classification of groups can be drawn up using many different kinds of base criteria. Thus a group can be defined according to its purpose, its activity, or the field of endeavour in which it is established, and finally according to the principal theory of human behaviour which motivates the group's direction. These various approaches to the classification of groups will now be looked at in some detail.

Classification by purpose

Created groups are established to achieve all kinds of purposes and they can thus be classified accordingly. If, for instance, a group has been established in order to pass on certain information, as might well be the case with a group in an educational establishment, then a whole order of groups can be established which have this as a basic purpose. Now it should be quite clear that this purpose may be arrived at by the use of the group in significantly different ways. Thus the information to be shared could be handed out in a didactic teaching fashion or imparted in some other way, or the information if it were of a different kind could be a matter of people talking about their experiences in order that they could pool the information that they possessed between them. The purpose of the group is the same in each instance but the approach is necessarily different. In the first case the information is available and is given out as it were, in the second it has to be drawn out as a contribution by each of the members.

Groups can therefore be created for a wide variety of purposes. They can be used for the achievement of learning, of therapy, of leisure activities, or to create personal growth. In short wherever it is deemed possible that people working together can achieve some task or some beneficial end, then it would be true to say that a group can be created.

Classification by activity

What the group does is just as effective a method of classing it as that using purpose. For those people who believe that groups have only one activity, that is to talk, this may come as something of a surprise. But groups are set up where the main activity is play, or work, or movement, or touch, or recreation. To complicate matters even more, these various activities are frequently used in some combination in order to maximize their effects. Thus working with young people it may be advisable to start a group with some form of physical activity which will then provide the necessary source of situations for them to talk about, largely because of the recency of the experience.

Classification by the field of endeavour

Obviously groups are used in different fields of human endeavour. Groups are to be found in hospitals, schools, factories, teaching institutions, theatres, social work agencies, churches hostels, clinics etc. The basic purpose of such groups will most clearly be to forward in some explicit way the general purpose of the institution or endeavour in which it is located. A group which is to be found in say a halfway house for persons discharged from a psychiatric unit will be a group within the field of rehabilitation in psychiatry. The activity which may be primarily used could be role play and the purpose to prepare the members in an indirect way for the resumption of life in the community.

Classification by theory

This kind of classification is dependent upon a group being based upon either a particular approach to the understanding of human behaviour in general, or on a particular approach to the way in which groups are believed to work. Psychological theories account for the largest number of the ways of classification here. Thus if the person who establishes a group tends to believe that Gestalt psychology has a great deal to offer in coping with the kind of problem with which his group is in existence to deal, or even if he should believe that Gestalt methods are most compatible with his way of working, then clearly the kind of group that he will set up will be very different from the group which might have been set up by another group leader to meet the same problem but who operated from a different theoretical base.

Of course this outline has barely skimmed the surface of the possible ways of classifying groups. One thing must be obvious and that is that all these ways are not mutually exclusive. In fact any one group can be defined many ways. Often in fact a group is defined using several forms, e.g. a psychoanalytically based therapy group using discussion and interpretation with psychiatric inpatients in a hospital setting. This example has in fact highlighted one of the main classification methods which has not been mentioned up to this point; that is classification by the kind of people who become the members of the group ... in this case inpatients in a psychiatric hospital.

What must be abundantly clear from what has gone so far is that the ideas, the philosophy, and the aims of the leader play a cardinal part in the kind of group which emerges. This is so whether the group is at one end of the directive scale or the other. If there is no absolute leader and members of the group are equally responsible for its destiny, then the prevailing ethos will determine which way the group goes. For the very simple reason that the norms and values of the group will dictate that wherever choice of direction exists that selected will be in accordance with those values.

There is no such thing as a leaderless group in the sense that no one exerts influence on others in order to direct the group in certain ways rather than in others.

This leads us to a consideration of the way in which radically different concepts about the ability of human beings leads to a very different approach to the use of groups. If one believes that there is a great deal of potential in each human being to develop and that the only way that this potential can be tapped is to create a situation in which the individual can grow, then one's approach to working with groups will be very different from that which would arise if one also believed that potential can be realized by a paternalistic approach as as we shall now see.

The group as context and as instrument

A very important distinction between groups is the one between context and instrument. Now this piece of jargon represents a distinction which many people find very hard to grasp, although it represents a real difference. The difference is not just one of the way the group happens to be run but a much more fundamental distinction of philosophy.

A group can be set up in which the basic aim is that each individual works with the leader on achieving the member's own individual goals. The rest of the group form a background to this endeavour and each takes this position with the leader in his turn. Many therapy groups are run on exactly these lines. The group here is said to be the *context* of treatment. Another group may be set up in which the leader tries to establish a situation in which all the members come to trust one another sufficiently to want to work together as a unit. The leader is not unduly predominant and each member feels that he has some degree of responsibility for the rest of the group as well as for himself. In this case the group is said to be the *instrument* of treatment.

In the first instance the group is merely an accessory. The real work is done between the individual member and the leader

32

who has to be a person of great skill and understanding. What members of the group who are not directly engaged stand to gain by being present can be stated fairly easily. First, they are able to see the resolution of a problem or problems which may well bear some direct resemblance to their own. Thus they stand to learn by seeing the way it is handled and also by a process known as *contagion* to pick up some of the relief that the individual being dealt with is actually feeling. There can be a great sense of understanding and of a burden lifted when it can be demonstrated that such a problem can in fact be coped with.

Second, the sense of sharing in the process of problem relief beings good feelings and trust of the leader tends to develop quite quickly. There is of course the problem that such trust may go too far and become a dependency. In fact one of the major problems of this kind of approach is that the leaders are usually very skilled and charismatic persons and the result can often be the creation of a dependent state in which the group member is relieved of his difficulties only in the presence and with the support of the leader.

In the second kind of group the strength to help lies in the mutual support which the group can develop and not in the special expertise of the leader or of any other member or outside person. The group is not just a background against which two people perform, it becomes the actual instrument by which they learn to grow and to become self-sufficient.

The philosophy is quite different in each case. In one the assumption is paternalistic, i.e. the expert has spent a great deal of time in learning how to deal with people who have certain kinds of problems. He will therefore advise, interpret, and help from a position of strength — his superior knowledge and experience. In the other there is the assumption that no one can really help anyone else directly, people have to learn how best to help themselves. Another assumption which is made is that all people have the capacity to grow and to change for the better their way of life. And finally there is an assumption that when people are involved in a situation themselves they can have a far more essential knowledge of what such a situation actually

33

involves than can someone who has never experienced it. Of course this last assumption can be taken to extremes. But even so there is always the sense that people who have been through the fire know more accurately what it is like to be burned than someone who has watched from the sidelines. Shared experience can provide the basis for much rational and effective action in dealing with problems, provided that the shared experience is discovered in a supportive situation like a group.

One final point about these two approaches to groups is this. As we have seen, groups can and do apply pressures to their members. The value of these pressures can be their acceptance by the members when similar pressures exerted from without the group would be resisted. Group influence is very powerful and not to use it for beneficial ends seems to be wasteful. However it must be said that there are circumstances when one approach is more suitable than the other. For instance, with people who have no experience or understanding of groups who need security and strength to rely on as a child does on its parents, then the paternalistic approach provides this strength and this security. But when people need to grow, then they also need independence.

Now I think it is necessary that we should look at some different kinds of groups more closely to see what they consist of and how they are arrived at. The family has already been discussed as the peculiar kind of group that it is and there is thus no need to elaborate further here, except to say that the family can be approached theoretically in many different ways, though the outcomes are usually of the order of making it function more effectively as a group.

Committees

Any committee is a very good example of a task-oriented group with a very clear set of rules about procedure and sometimes even a very set form of speech. The main task of a committee is to make decisions and for this reason and because it is much organized a committee makes a good example to study. The lines, which occur in any group, are so clearly drawn and so formalized here that it becomes easier to see how they can occur in much less clear form in other groups.

Committees work on the basic premise that a given number of people will produce a more considered approach to the solution of a problem or arrive at a more balanced decision than an individual or even a smaller number of people. The evidence for the truth of this assertion is nowhere really disputed. 'More people, more ideas' is obviously true. What is needed is the kind of structure which allows those ideas to be expressed and to be considered in the light of their worth to the solution of the problem in consideration. This is where the rules of procedure become very necessary. All information and discussion is offered through the chair based upon the fact that if all communication nets are routed through one central point, then whoever occupies that point has overall control of the communication flow.

The role of the chairman is therefore crucial to the success of this method of group use. His role represents a strictly directive form of leadership which is again a very logical way to proceed when it is realized that committees have only a limited time in which to come to a decision. As will be continually stressed here, all groupwork is essentially a very logical situation which takes cognizance of what is to be achieved and the ways available to achieve it and balances them out to make the most effective working compromise. Thus given a limited time and a decision to reach, a skilfully directive leadership and a set of known rules by which all agree to abide are essential for success.

Michael Argyle reviewing the factors which make a committee most effective noted five. First, members should possess the knowledge and skills appropriate to the job in hand; second, they should be co-operative rather than competitive; third, they should be able to stimulate one another to produce creative ideas; fourth, the chairman should demonstrate leadership skills of a high order directing the group to co-ordinate its efforts, allow the expression of minority feelings, prevent conformity pressures producing inferior decisions, and help the group to arrive at acceptable decisions; fifth, the size of the committee

35

should be relevant to the task it has in hand.[4]

If we are concerned to learn about the ways in which groups work so that we can use those ways for beneficial ends, then the clear design of the committee is a good example of how this can be done. The structure tends to be clear, the rules are evident, the leadership is unambiguous, and the purpose of the group clearly outlined.

When we turn to other kinds of groups, it is well to realize that the same factors are operating but that they may in no way appear to be so obvious to the observer. The skill of being a group worker is to have reached a point where they are as obvious in all groups.

The family is what is called a natural group, the committee is not. It is a created group. For the most part this book will be concerned with created groups, that is groups which are set up to achieve a given purpose or purposes. One of the most important growth areas of groupwork over the last few years has been that concerned with achieving personal growth.

We have seen earlier how people are dependent upon the response they elicit from others for confirmation not only *of* but also *for* knowledge of their behaviour patterns. If one believes that there is potential in every human being to enhance the efficacy of those behaviour patterns, then the first step would seem to be the need to get clear what the patterns are and then to make some attempt to modify them. Groups based upon this theme are now very numerous which is a sad comment upon the kind of society which makes such expedients necessary.

Where one's behaviour is reflected back to one by others in a group whom one tends to, or has learnt to, trust, then there is a great chance that one will accept that reflection as indicating the truth. With help from those selfsame people one can then decide to change or not. This means clearing away a lot of the debris which growing up in society has encumbered us with, enabling us to become more open and honest, in other words to

4 Michael Argyle, *Social Interaction* London, Methuen, 1970, pp.259-60. The whole of this section (pp.240-66) called 'Five kinds of small social group' is well worth reading.

become more childlike in our outlook. The leadership in a group of this nature is very skilled indeed and needs to be directed to achieving situations in which the group members feel free enough of their normal inhibitions to be able to discuss themselves openly and of course to talk about others in the same way.[5]

Groups have traditionally been used for the treatment of people, especially those deemed to be suffering from some form of mental illness, for a very long time. Here the emphasis is sometimes on the curative factor of the group itself and at others on the skills, knowledge, and understanding of the therapist. The basic difference of these approaches has been outlined elsewhere in this book.

Groups have always been used for leisure activities, in team pastimes especially, and for the enjoyment of other people's company. Work shows often enough the need for people to co-operate to achieve the end product and in virtually every area of life we are faced with groups operating. Almost every area of human experience has been and is subjected to group experience, communal living, sexual behaviour, learning etc., etc. Because 'groupness' is such a common factor of natural living it is used to enhance life in purposeful ways.

Group development

A very confusing state of affairs exists in the literature about the idea of group development largely because development is dynamic and the whole concept can be regarded as a process in the same way that photography is a process. This means that in many texts on working with groups, the use of the word 'process' means the way the group grows and changes, an overview of its history, and the word is always singular.

Now I have referred to 'processes' in the plural in chapter

5 Many texts have been written about this use of groups to facilitate personal growth and many different approaches are practised. I would recommend that *Learning and Change in Groups* by Arthur Blumberg and Robert Golembiewski published by Penguin books 1976 be used as a starter.

3 because I believe that the way a group develops is only one process among several which are generated. However as the idea of development is very important, the use of 'process' in the singular will be retained where appropriate.

Why is development in a group so important and what does it really mean? Well a group can be regarded as a unit which is constantly changing largely because the ways in which its members interact with one another change as they change. New experiences, different moods, perceptions, and understanding are both brought from outside into the group and created within the group to be used outside it.

When this interchange does not occur we quite rightly say that the group has stagnated. This state of affairs can sometimes be seen among collections of old people where no stimulus from outside is brought in and the group itself generates none. People become apathetic and routine-bound and if this goes on for a long period of time, will come to lose the facility to change and will often in fact resent change which will cause them first, to recognize their state and second, to put out some effort to change it.

The fact that stimulated groups change is one thing, to say that they develop implies that there is some perceptible order or direction about the change and this is precisely what group theorists imply when they talk about the developmental stages of a group. To most people the stages defined by the specialists could almost all be covered by the idea of increased familiarity — a kind of getting used to people and to a letting down of hair. This is, as far as it goes, quite perceptive.

What development can also be likened to is the maturation process of the child as he gradually learns about himself and his abilities and about the environment which surrounds him including those important adults. Neither is it a totally accurate picture, because the group which develops is a unit comprising separate individuals who recognize more or less clearly that in order to achieve whatever ends the group was created for, they will have to come to terms with individual differences and learn to co-operate to an appropriate level.

38

Development then in a group implies that all groups which survive move towards a more efficient use of their resources. Many people have attempted to define what this development looks like and to suggest that it occurs in stages. While I would agree that there appear to be well-marked points in the life of any group, I am in no way convinced that group development is a straightforward procedure with stage two appearing some time after stage one has been consolidated. Experience shows some very interesting facts:

1 Some groups hardly show any development — maybe it is not necessary to achieve their purpose, maybe they have not the potential. There may be many reasons both internal and external.

2 Development is patchy in several ways:

(a) Some people in a group see and feel the need to change before others and bring pressure to bear on them to follow suit — this sometimes results in some individuals, who may appear to be holding the group back, being subjected to quite strong aggression.

(b) Some groups seem to fluctuate in that they make progress and then regress and seem to need to win some of their ground over again. This can occur when the group as it were outgrows its own strength and in order to consolidate has to regress to a previous safe point and rebuild slowly.

(c) Some areas of group behaviour develop more quickly and soundly than others. For instance a group of strangers can sometimes discover something that they all have in common, beyond their common humanity that is, which very quickly develops a sense of being in the same boat. The actual understanding of each other as people may in no way have kept pace with this emotional warmth generated by the similarity and it is sometimes very easily demonstrated to be a false dawn when the group is offered pressure commensurate with its apparent level of development.

3 Different stages in the development of a group allow the group to cope with different kinds of stress. This point will be elaborated later in terms of the difference between a group which is just a collection of people and a 'formed' group in which a stage of development has been reached which is consonant with the group's being able to work as a unit. Before this stage the group could be said to be composed of individuals whose prime motivation was their personal security and advantage, and the security or advantage of the group trailed a long way behind. After this stage, the group becomes much more equal and deserving of consideration and eventually the bond may become so strong that the individual member's advantage is placed well behind the sought-for advantage for the group.

This can mean that the sort of pressure which a group can tolerate may well be related to the stage of its development, a point which should not go unnoticed by potential group leaders. Incidentally when a task can be performed by individuals as members of a group then there is a very real danger that unless what they do is integrated into the group's pattern it will begin to create gaps between the members. There are many so-called groups in which there are doers and hangers-on or watchers — in reality two groups with very different levels of satisfaction from membership.

Development usually implies growth and growth implies the achievement of an ultimate state. In the case of closed groups or groups with a limited life span, achievement may well be followed by death in the natural pattern. Open groups with no limit do not of course die but they are constantly renewed, only the individual members whose purpose has been fulfilled by membership or whose circumstances make such membership either no longer possible or desirable separate from the parent unit.

So the process of development is in reality the history of the life of the group charted and showing some kind of generalized movement towards increased efficiency over a period of time if healthy, and eventually ceasing to exist when the reasons for its creation have been achieved or have changed. Much will be said later about the way in which groups can be encouraged to develop to the point where they can work at the job in hand and even about the ways in which they can be closed when the task is complete, leaving a sense of achievement, a spirit of co-operation, and an enhanced understanding of self and others, however small, as a bonus.

3 The basic characteristics of its members

In discussing the many different kinds of groups which are in use today it must have become obvious that I was also inferring that there were certain similarities about all groups. This is perhaps the main point about understanding what groups are and what they can do. Put simply it means that every group really has the same basic ingredients available to it, but that they are either not used in the same way, or in the same order, or that some are stressed and others are not and so on.

At the risk of being accused of being too simple, it must be stated that the basic form of any group is that a collection of people are together for a period of time in a given place. Now we know that when people gather together in a place where they can see one another and become aware of each other's presence that their behaviour tends to start to take account of the presence of others. It is the ways in which this behaviour manifests itself which form the basic characteristics of any group, and further-more what kind of behaviour actually emerges will depend to a great extent on the previous experience of similar situations which the members of the group will have had in the past. This means that the whole of their relevant experience of which they are more or less aware will be brought into play in order that they will feel rather safer. For as we have seen, the fear, the basic fear of being forced to regard oneself as an isolate and alone, is sufficient to make us try very hard to reduce strange and new situations to something which is less strange and more comfortable and liveable with.

So all groups produce what can be called processes, that is movements which tend to make for greater psychic comfort on the part of the members. A great deal will be said about this at a later stage when we need to look at the fact that a collection of people is not a group in the sense of being a unit. There is quite a large element of time involved before the strangers in any group can have shared sufficient experience with their new colleagues to allow them to feel able to relax the guards they have erected for their defence. Defences, as we shall see, consume energy which could otherwise be used in working together. Because all groups produce processes all groups could be called 'process groups'.

Process groups

What I have called process groups are not a special kind of group in the sense that a work group is devoted to work. Rather it is a kind of shorthand for a special, and I believe basic, way of looking at and attempting to understand any group.

Wherever a collection of people exists as such over a period of time, then inevitably certain things will occur even if it is just a recognition of the fact that the collection exists and that each individual sees himself in some discrete way as belonging to it, or part of it. In a way this recognition does not even require a basic commitment on the part of the individual except to be there with all the others. It does not even require his willingness to be there, though there is a much greater chance of what has been called a 'formed' group developing, if his physical presence is accompanied by a degree of commitment to the collection of individuals.

It must now be clear that whatever factors distinguish a group of individuals from a solitary individual, including the factor of existence over a period of time, may be said to be the defining features of a group. If these features are found in any other kind of collectivity to the same degree or intensity, then either that collectivity is some form of group or the factors we have accepted as defining are not specific enough. The fact that a group in order to exist at all and to be recognized needs to continue over a period of time makes it inevitable that all the factors which will identify a group are liable to be processes, i.e. factors which develop through time and exposure.

In fact so important has the concept of development over time been to those who analyse groups, that it has frequently been treated as if it were the single important factor in the understanding of group behaviour. In one sense this is true, i.e. in that groups have to exist over time and that what they do can thus be seen in the context of a time sequence. But what is it that develops or changes over time? Some people would argue that it is the interaction of the members, i.e. their communication with one another, their awareness of each other, and so on. Indisputably this is correct. But is this all? Of course not! There are at least ten processes which operate in any group and which with a little practice anyone can identify. This means that we are looking at the group as a functioning unit and attempting to see actually what is happening. It is a fairly short, though sometimes difficult, step from recognizing what is happening to the realization that the processes may be either helping the group to achieve whatever end it has set for itself or they may be actively hindering such achievement. Logically intervention to ensure that those processes which are facilitating the group's achievement are enhanced and the others reduced is the next move. Such intervention can, of course, be undertaken by any member of a group who is aware of what is involved. It may well be that the aim of a particular group is to try to ensure that any member is aware enough of what is going on to intervene in this way.

If group development and interaction between members are only two of the processes, what are the other eight? Well any group develops what may be called a social structure. This means that the behaviour of certain individuals in relation to the group occurs with sufficient frequency to become definite and thus to confirm the social position of those members. For example, if a group member habitually takes over the role of conciliator, then his social role becomes confirmed, that is the other members have some fair level of expectancy that he will fulfil that role. The degree of stability these roles possess equates with the visible level of social structure. Confirmed alliances between members, consistent use of power, high or low status are all forms of structure.

If alliances become fairly permanent or even recognizable, then the process of sub-group formation has taken place.

Most if not all groups have a purpose, more or less recognized, as the reason for their existence. Purposes change over time and the process of forming goals which the members accept is universal in groups even if the acceptance is either a form of collusion or a tacit understanding or the result of apathy. The process of decision-making is involved here as it is in most of the group's activities.

All groups tend to set norms and standards of behaviour if not openly in the form of explicit rules, then covertly in the form of role models and by the non-acceptance of non-conforming behaviour. Likewise all groups develop a level of attractiveness for their members. This process develops a bond between members, an awareness of their togetherness, and of their belonging.

Of course all groups exert pressure on their members and usually the level of pressure or influence can be greater if the level of satisfaction of the members is high. Finally, groups develop what can be described as a 'climate', an atmosphere which is recognizable in the same way that the characteristics of an individual are recognizable as cheerful or miserable.

Obviously all of these processes are not of the same order of event. Indeed they are of at least four different kinds. They can be classified as follows:

Basic	Structural	Achieving	Influencing
Interaction	Development	Goal formation	Norms
	Social structure	Decision-making	Standards and
	Sub-group		values
	formation		Cohesion
			Influence
			Climate

In the sense that all groups display these processes all groups are 'process' groups. But the point at issue is not that the processes exist, but whether they are recognized as such and used.

Before looking at the group processes in some detail, it is necessary to mention briefly what may be referred to as the constraints. All groups whether natural or created exist in an environment. Now that may sound so obvious as not to need saying. But unfortunately this is not true. Many groups have been created which in many ways ignore or at least tend to ignore the environment into which they are born.

Much will be said later about the effects of the constraints both in creating and in running a group. All that needs to be said here as a first introduction to the idea is that many factors: the environment, the resources available, the time, the skills, the qualities of the members etc., all have great effect upon the group and upon the outcomes which are possible. In this sense groupwork is the art of the possible and an effective group worker is able to make a realistic assessment of the possible effect that any given factors which come within the ambit of his group will tend to have on it. Thus although it may be desirable to attempt to achieve a certain end for a given group of people, it may not be possible because of the constraints which exist and other aims may have to be substituted. Of course all constraints are neither negative in their effects nor are they necessarily unsupportive. In most cases recognition of their existence is recognition of reality, and aims can be designed which are not only beneficial but possible. It also needs to be recognized that some constraints can be changed by the application of suitable pressure.

Any collection of people therefore which exists as such over a period of time is subject to two major influences. First, the processes which stem from the awareness that each individual has of the presence of the others and consequently of the responses which he will tend to produce, and second, all those pressures which arise from the fact that the collection of people does not exist in a vacuum but is part of larger organizations and comprises people who belong to other groups as well.

What happens in a group?

When people are aware that there are others within the same local area as themselves, they react to the presence of those others in a variety of ways. What those ways are does not really concern us too much here, but the fact that reaction does take place does. If the reaction is one of attempting to ignore the others, it must be recognized that this reaction is brought about by the recognition of their presence. We do not make efforts to ignore things when we are totally unaware of their existence.

Depending on how we feel towards the others in our space so the reactions will be tempered. The degree of our need to be accepted by them for instance will be a great factor in the kind of attitude we will display.

If we take a group of people who are brought together because they are facing a common problem, whatever that might be, then before they can begin to operate as a group a whole large area of safety needs to be cleared up. During the course of talking together the members of a group like this will begin to use established ways of assuring themselves that what they have come into is going to be beneficial for them. They are going to form impressions about the other members of the group and they are going to have feelings ranging from liking to disliking, and from suspicion to trust. They are going to try to establish what their own position in the group is liable to be and whether it is one which will carry sufficient reward to be worth the risks which may be involved. All this and much more occurs because the people involved will interact with one another, they will

47

communicate with each other, they will weigh one another in the scales of past experience, and they will make judgements.

Now one of the reasons for bringing together a group of people who have a common problem is very simple; it is that they will all have tried in some way or other to find a solution or way of coping with the problem. Of course some will have been more successful than others and some may have been totally defeated by the problem. If it now becomes possible for the people in the group to share their experiences of the ways in which they coped or did not cope, then each can learn something which may be of value and help in their own coping. So this is obvious and it would seem reasonable to bring it about. Why doesn't it happen without the necessity of someone creating the opportunity? Well of course it does in many instances, but in many others it does not for the very simple reason that people are not usually very aware that others are in the same boat as themselves. Or if they are they are not sure of how they would be received if they tried to do something about it.

Quite a lot of these attitudes still remain when people with common problems are brought together by someone who is aware of their common difficulty. Given that sharing experience can increase the available coping behaviours for the sharers, a group can create the interaction necessary for an appropriate level of trust to develop so that the exchange can take place.

Interaction is the basic common process of all groups. People talk to each other, they relate their experiences, they watch each other, they smile, frown, laugh, cry, and perhaps touch one another. Gradually through this interaction they come to form opinions about each other and may well come to recognize that they are not as different or as isolated or as incompetent as they had thought.

In order for the collection of people to be able to achieve this level of appreciation of the worth of themselves and of the others, the process has to be regulated in some way. Most often what happens is that the standards of the society in which the majority of the members exist are brought into the group. For example standards of politeness in allowing other people to finish what they have to say and of not rudely interrupting. However these standards tend to be modified as the group finds what suits its needs best. It has in fact created its own norms and standards of behaviour. There may have been no conscious decision about the behaviours which are acceptable, but nevertheless commonly agreed norms will emerge and those whose behaviour transgresses these norms will feel other members of the group expressing their disapproval in a variety of ways, which usually amount to some kind of withdrawal of acceptance of the offending member.

During the course of the group's existence, certain members will come to accept and to be given particular jobs to do. If these jobs become an acceptable part of the group's behaviour, then the process of creating a structure within the group will have occurred. For instance there may be one person within a group who always seems to be the one to whom others turn when they are hurt, or there may be someone who can always be relied upon to ensure that time limits are observed and appears to be very conscious of the need to get on with whatever task is in hand. These roles become identifiable because they tend to be performed often enough to become somewhat predictable and also expected. When this happens, then the group has a social structure which can be recognized not only by those within the group but also by any percipient outsider.

One fact must have emerged from all of the foregoing and that is how extremely important the element of time is in every one of the processes so far discussed. Groups change, some would say that they grew, over time. As the members begin to have more and more shared experience with each other, particularly if this experience has been pleasant or valuable or both, then their relationships change and the group as a whole moves into a different phase of its existence. The process of development is well documented in the groupwork literature and in fact some group workers use the developmental sequence in their attempts to produce groups whose members have some problem with making relationships with others.

Of course in the process of being together members of a group will discover affinities with other members and so will tend to band together for support. Sub-groups will thus form around people or ideas and provided they are not too opposed to the main stream of objectives of the whole group, it is from such groups that most of the new ideas and the inspirations tend to come. This is not to say that an individual with good ideas cannot also influence the group to a great extent, but unless he is very strong or a very much respected member of the group he will usually tend to seek support for his ideas from others and then a sub-group will have to come into existence. Some sub-groups become permanent, others are ephemeral merely serving the current needs of those who form them. They also form the possible basis of rebellion and of opting out, because they can support individuals to the point where they feel strong enough to resist the group.

All groups which survive make decisions about what they exist to do. In some cases these decisions are made by individuals who for one reason or another are strong or who feel that they are more aware of what is needed. But even in cases like these there is an obvious need to be able to carry the rest of the group, or at least some significant part of it, along with the decision. What develops then is a process of making decisions within the group. In order to maintain the satisfaction of members at a high level they need to feel that they have some say in what the group is going to do. Nothing causes people in any organisation to feel redundant quicker than to realize that all the important decisions in their group life are made by others.

Decisions are made about procedure, about the rules of behaviour, about organization, admissions to the group, and about the thousand-and-one details of the daily running of the group. But above all decisions are made about what the group is in being to achieve. So a process of deciding what the group is about becomes another common denominator in any group.

The goals or purposes of the group may be of many kinds. They may comprise goals which individual members of the group find important for themselves, there may be goals which the organizers and supporters of the group have in mind, there may be goals which members have in mind for the whole group, and there may be goals which are spaced in time usually called proximate and long-term goals. Obviously if a degree of chaos exists about all these sources of goals, then the group will soon cease to exist as a group and nothing will have been achieved except disappointment. Thus part of the early work of any collection of people hoping to become a group must be to try to sort out what kind of aims each member has for himself and for the group as a whole. This is easier said than done for two very simple reasons. First, most of us tend to believe that what we understand to be the reason for a group's existence is the same as what everybody else believes. After all we obtained it from the same available sources. This of course is false because we have not allowed for the element of interpretation which we all place upon even the simplest information. Thus even in a well-organized group set-up, the potential members will be there for substantially different reasons as well as the common ones, and this needs to be allowed for.

Second, members may not be prepared to divulge the expectations they have of the group because for some reason or other they do not want the rest of the group to know. Usually this is because either they are ashamed that others should know their reasons and dislike them, for there is some realization that the reasons may be different in kind or quality from those advanced by the others. For instance many people attend group sessions as part of the in-service training programme of the organization for which they work. Now they may well have no great faith that they will learn anything from this process, but to admit this would put them in bad odour with the organization and would also deprive them of the possibility of having a period of time away from the daily routine. So such motives tend to be hidden behind a façade of being present and having the same goals as the others. However these hidden expectations can in fact sabotage the whole group's learning and need to be brought out into the open where they can be considered as part of what the group has to cope with. In any case as motives they exist and therefore they are as valid as any others.

When all such motives can be brought out into the open the group has gone a long way towards creating a basic atmosphere of trust and understanding in which other risks can, and will, be taken, as we shall see later. People who have been in many groups are quite able to talk about the different climates which are engendered by groups. Some are friendly, some are deadly serious, some work hard, others seem to get just as much done with an atmosphere of lightheartedness and fun being the main climate and so on. Of course what the group is doing may well have some bearing on the kind of climate which is engendered, but this is not solely the cause. Most groups, if they are effective, tend to develop the climate which is conducive to the completion of the task they have in hand. Non-effective groups tend to have climates which fluctuate wildly and which frequently interfere with the purpose of the group.

Over a period of time group members come to feel a kind of emotional bond for their fellow members. It is compounded of many emotions and is based upon having shared a considerable number of experiences with them. This bond tends to divide those who are members of the group from those who are not. A point which all who work with groups need to take into very serious consideration, i.e. group membership is an exclusive as well as inclusive activity. Group bond shows a feeling of attraction that members have about their group and also as a sense of belonging and of deriving support from the group. When this occurs the group is usually described as being cohesive.

Groupwork literature tends to overemphasize the value of this factor. Granted it is very important, but it has negative aspects, as for instance when a group becomes so cohesive that it stagnates as no outside influence or breath of fresh thinking can penetrate its exclusive boundaries. Of course there is also the possibility that a very cohesive group can maintain bad ideas and standards with exactly the same fervour as we expect other groups will generate good ones.

Finally in this discussion of the factors that all groups have in common there is the factor of influence. From what has already been said it must be obvious that the reason that groups are effective in supporting and in changing the behaviour of individuals is because a group is able to exert some pressure on its members. The greater the need an individual has of being accepted by a group the greater the pressure that group can exert upon him, providing that there are no known and possible alternatives. Obviously if a group means little to an individual, then if the pressure to do what the group wishes him to do becomes too great he will cut his dissatisfactions and leave. If he happens to be in a group from which this is not possible, i.e. in a prison or treatment group with penalties for withdrawal, then his leaving will take the form of psychological withdrawal rather than physical.

Of course if groups were not able to bring this kind of pressure to bear upon their members, then there would be no valid reason for using groups for any kind of therapeutic, change, or leisure purposes except in so far as they would still be able to achieve things which were beyond the capability of the individual. Then such groups would be entirely temporary, existing merely to the completion of the task.

I hope that it is now clear that, although we started from the idea of the diversity of groups, all groups have got an enormous number of things in common most of which derive from the fact that we have been brought up in group situations and that we spend by far the greater part of our lives as members of all kinds of groups. Of course some of these groups are transient, but some like the family exist and influence us all our lives. Many other groups have this effect also, though it is infrequent that we are as aware of this influence and of our need to be accepted which makes us so conforming even when we think we are rebelling. Immediately others rebel with us we form a conforming group of rebels. We can be recognized by the aspects of our conformity.

We must now turn to look at what it is that makes the difference between a collection of people who have the potential to become a group, and a group which is truly 'formed'.

There is then the need to recognize the fact that no group

exists in a vacuum. In every sense a group is part of the milieu in which it is founded. It both influences and is influenced by its surroundings.

It is therefore no use expecting that a group can be applied to remedy a situation in the same way that a piece of sticking plaster can be applied to a minor wound. If the analogy is to be followed up, the sticking plaster would have to become an integral part of the wound and the wound a part of the plaster. This is mainly what is meant when the textbooks on groupwork refer to the constraints within which groups exist.

The constraints

Constraints are all those factors which can affect the creation, life, and outcome of a group. This is not to say that the effects are all negative and restrictive, quite the contrary. Some constraints are positive and very useful. The essential fact about constraints however is that they need to be recognized and taken into consideration when planning the group, and their ongoing influence needs constant monitoring during the life of the group.

> A group of teenage probationers was set up by their probation officer to meet on a weekly basis in a room at the local college of education. While geographically the college was a good choice, it was unfortunate in that it was unfamiliar to the lads in the group and made them feel uncomfortable and very conscious of their status of being, as they put it, 'cons'. Their behaviour became defiant and for some long period of time they were unable to settle down to the task of the group.

This was a small example of the effect that environment can have on the performance of a group. The site had been chosen by the group leader because it was very convenient for all those involved. The amenities were good, but the essential fact of being not only unfamiliar ground to the lads but also a place connected with higher education had not been allowed for in the original group design. It proved unsettling enough to cause the group to end prematurely.

Time

Time is one of the most important of the constraints in several ways. There is the amount of time available for each session, the time between sessions, and the time that the group will run. All these factors need to be taken into consideration when a group is being planned. The example quoted below is from a report by a group of social workers on a groupwork project with children.

> Social workers were expected to involve themselves in the group in their own leisure time with no lessening of their commitments elsewhere. This meant that the social workers were often tired and lacking in enthusiasm, which can only prevent groups from reaching their full potential... Other important factors which relate to the success or failure of groupwork are proper communications with parents, schools and other social workers, full discussion of each meeting and written reports. Time was scarce and for us this meant that all these areas were neglected to some degree and not really satisfactorily dealt with.

Time here reduced the possible effectiveness because the amounts of it that were essential to achieve success were not forthcoming. It is a common problem of groupwork that leaders underestimate the amount of time that will have to be made available to do the job properly.

Another group from the same project also found that time was an important factor and the extract from their report quoted below shows how much time they had to devote to their group.

> Wednesday evenings over the six months have involved approximately eighty hours work for each social worker. Added to this are three weekends and one Saturday, as well as many hours, mainly within normal working time spent discussing the group and planning. Without taking the weekends into consideration, this represents a conservative estimate of ten per cent increase on each social worker workload.

55

Time shows its major effect in the development of a 'formed' group from a collection of people who are occupying the same geographical space.

Formed groups

Many references will be made in the course of this book to something called a 'formed' group. In essence this term is used only of groups which have been together as a group for a period of time long enough for certain things to have happened.

When people collect together for whatever purpose then certain events start to occur. Some people with some experience of leading groups may make efforts to run the group along the lines that they think appropriate, based upon their past experience. Others tend to resist this kind of approach because they do not like the idea of being told what to do. They may not however make any other constructive suggestion about what can be done. Still others in the group will see their role as soothers and smoothers — maybe this is where they have found themselves to be most useful in the past.

Whatever the people who comprise the group will do, all the processes, almost without exception, which make up the peculiar dynamic of a small group will be functioning in some form or other right from the start. Unless there is someone in the collection of people who has a certain knowledge of what makes a group able to stay and work together, then none of the processes will be particularly emphasized at the expense of the others.

Such a group may well decide to elect various members to positions of authority within the group, on the basis of this being a well tried method of obtaining co-operative endeavour between several people. But the major fact is that this group cannot be what is termed a 'formed' group until each and every member of it is aware of the fact that he belongs to the group and that he gets some satisfaction from that membership.

The key distinction between a 'formed' group and any other stage in the development of a group is that the members have developed a degree of trust in each other and in their group which is appropriate to the task they have in hand. This concept is crucial to the effective functioning of task-oriented groups. What is more, the period of time which is usually allowed for this kind of trust to develop is more often than not far too short.

A 'formed' group then is one in which the members have been in contact with one another for long enough for most of the problems of relationships to have been sorted out and thus no longer disruptive of working harmony. The period of time reqired to accomplish this state may be as long as twelve contact hours, i.e. hours spent entirely in each other's company as members of the group however separated by time spent elsewhere.

One frequent result of ignoring this fact is that groups newly created are asked to work, i.e. to co-operate in the performance of some task, and they find that this is not possible. Energy which should be devoted to the group task is being devoted to the needs of personal security. In very simple terms the group has not had time to settle down to form relationships appropriate to the task and is thus not a 'formed' group and cannot work as such. Individuals within the group may well try to accomplish the set task, but the group will only be able to do it when it has become a group.

The period before the forming of the group is usually referred to graphically as the 'shakedown' period and requires very careful handling by the group leader. He can of course use his influence and various techniques to ensure that the 'shakedown' period is no longer than it need be. These will be discussed and illustrated in the section on operation.

Other constraints are the members themselves; the resources the group has at its disposal; the size of the group; whether the group assumes an open or closed state; the criteria of selection of the members which will obviously result in the exclusion of some and the admission of others; the activities the group chooses to follow; the nature of any contracts established and finally the kinds of intevention made by the leader or any other group member. The one constraint dealt with here is 'size', the others will be covered in chapters 4 and 5.

Size

Obviously the size of a group has some effect upon the way in which it works. Take just a very simple example: if a group has a given period of time in which to perform a particular task, say to come to a particular decision, then the amount of time which each member has to get his ideas across is a function of three main things, the organization of the group, the forcefulness or otherwise of the individual members, and of time. The latter because if all members are to contribute what they think, then the time will need to be equally divided. If therefore there are many members, the amount of time each has is small; if there are forceful members, many others may be deprived of what they would regard as their time and so on.

Thus if a group is large there is the possibility of more ideas being produced, but equally there is the chance that the time in which these ideas will be expressed will not be available unless some form of agreement or leadership is used to ensure just this. Alternatively if a group is small, there may be fewer ideas but there will be more time in which to express them.

These are obviously general ideas, for so far we have given no indication of what is small and what is large. Like most things concerned with groups this is a matter of what is appropriate. Thus small in one context is large in another. Generally speaking where the intensity of personal contact is important then groups of up to about fifteen may be considered, more intense personal contact will require even smaller groups. This is merely a function of the number of people that it is possible to contact on a face-to-face basis. Where the activity of the group is general and social the group can be much larger. Large groups always tend to split into smaller ones anyway if the activity that they are indulging in seems to warrant it. Large groups of up to forty, fifty, and upwards usually possess all the characteristic bonds of smaller groups when they are moved by intense feeling or absorption in their task. Of course this applies to much vaster groups, as any politician can aver, when emotion can weld a group to action despite its very cumbersome size.

Practical facts of number are few then except for things like odd numbers favouring reaching a decision on a voting basis, large groups providing the possibility of hiding for those members who do not want to take a prominent part in the proceedings, and small numbers generally intensifying the amount of personal contact that can take place. One other point needs to be mentioned and that is that very large groups have problems of communication and usually need some kind of structure or formal communication system. They also make it possible for members to come and go without affecting the culture of the group very much, being big enough to absorb, almost without noticing, the comings and goings of members.

Thus the size of a group has certain effects upon its possible performance and when creating a group it should be born in mind that some sizes are more appropriate to certain situations than others. There are no hard and fast rules about this but a simple matter of weighing up what the factors involved are and coming to a sensible decision in the light of what it is hoped to achieve.

4 Participant, member, director, audience

Perhaps one of the most written about but least understood areas of group behaviour is the function of the leader. If a group is to be created for a specific purpose then the acts of leadership are of paramount importance.

Traditionally the leader has been seen as one who possessed certain characteristics of leadership. The ability to influence the behaviour of others for example, or the ability to command respect, or just some natural gift which allowed the person who possessed it to take control of situations which other people could not control. Thus people who are concerned to become group leaders frequently ask what kind of characteristics are necessary in order to become good at the job.

Now it is without doubt that good leaders are usually possessed of intelligence, but this is in no way the same thing as saying that all people who possess intelligence will make good group leaders. In fact one of the most obvious facts about good group leaders is that they have received an adequate training in the skills of their profession. Given the fact that someone is interested in learning about group leadership, that he has the ability to see what is going on under his nose, and has some desire to do something about it, then the basic necessities of a good group leader are available.

What is more important than any innate ability is the way in which such a person can learn to observe and then to make some decision about the kind of action which will be most appropriate to the achieving of the operational aims of the group.

This chapter then is concerned with two major roles within the group that of the leader and that of the member. Of course these are not always easily distinguished and one person may well be playing both at any one time.

Leaders

The leader in the first instance is the person who makes some attempt to guide the group in the way which he sees as being important for it. Let us start right at the beginning and see what this means.

In chapter 2 we looked at the ways in which groups can originate. In nearly every way that was mentioned some one person or persons had to take some kind of responsibility for establishing that a group would be a good thing with which to meet some kind of situation. The implications behind this are so simple that most people take them for granted, but if we want to understand what is actually involved in this process then we cannot do this. The act is that of conceptualization which means that someone sees that there would be a need for the use of a group to achieve a certain end. In other words what they are saying is that having considered the situation it can best be met by the use of some form of group. If this insight does not occur, then no group will be formed. It is a recognition of the essential problems of a situation and of the nature of group processes.

Now this kind of leadership may not be connected directly with any skills in continuing leadership, as we shall see later. We have discussed at length why groups actually work and the processes which are involved. The act of conceptualization is deciding how best, if at all, these processes can be used to help some people establish a better approach to their lives or at least to some aspects of them.

There are many examples of this kind of thinking in the literature on groupwork so I will quote only one or two here as examples.

The Coventry City Centre Project identifies 'groups of young people who moved within the rather nebulous, provincial, drug subculture and either misused drugs or were "at risk"'.[1] Having done this the workers decided that some form of self-help group would be appropriate to this situation. What they actually came up with was a 'self-regulating co-operative of young people who are involved in identifying ways of helping each other with problems'.

In rural areas children frequently do not have the chance to meet one another and their parents likewise. Playgroups established in this kind of community offer a chance to both groups to meet, to socialize, and to provide a point of contact. Patients discharged from a psychiatric hospital may need some kind of support to enable them to adapt to life in the community after hospitalization and so on ... the list is endless.

Getting the first idea

A great deal of thinking needs to be gone through before any actual moves are made to establish a group. This process, usually referred to in the textbooks by the name of 'conceptualization' is one which tends to be bypassed by those who are very enthusiastic and who tend also to think that action is the most important part of the proceedings. Without doubt this is true, but if the ground work of thinking is not done well, then the action will not be very effective unless a great deal of luck is available.

The easiest way to approach the setting-up of a group is to ask a series of pertinent questions to which the answers should be at least fairly clear. The first of these questions is undoubtedly

1   Bob Rhodes, 'In Practice', *Community Care*, 25 February 1976, p.10.

'Why do I want to set up this group?' The answer may vary from 'Because I am excited about the idea of running a group' to a very clear statement on the lines of 'I want to run this group because I can see that there exists a collection of people who have at least one need which can be met most effectively by bringing them together so that they can share their experience of, say, some common problem'.

The second statement can only be made by someone who knows what a group has to offer. But sharing experiences is a very common reason for starting a group. Many people believe that their particular problem is absolutely unique to them, and they frequently get a great deal of support when they are placed in a situation where they realize that this is not true and they are not alone. In any case there is always the fact that when people have tackled a problem in isolation they have used the resources which they had available. These are very seldom the same for everyone, and the fact that they can be shared means that some people in a group will be exposed to ways of tackling their problem which had just never occurred to them before.

Some such idea of sharing forms the basis of many very successful groups and has the added force that when people have been in the same boat as others they are much more likely to accept that experience as genuine rather than the theoretical knowledge of the so called expert.

Many other questions need to be asked at this thinking stage, along the lines of 'Is it possible?', which is a question about resources, both material and in terms of skill. It is also a question about whether the time is available, whether the agency for which one works is really going to allow a group approach to its clients, and so on. Colleagues have to be consulted as their goodwill is absolutely necessary if the group is to get off the ground. All these factors are usually referred to as the 'constraints' and they will constantly recur during our consideration of working with groups of people. This is largely because poor consideration of the constraints and the ways in which they can affect the outcomes of a group are one of the main causes of failure.

It should be made clear at this stage that I am not advocating that the constraints should never be looked at in terms of their possible change. Some groups are set up with this as the express purpose of their existence. But it should always be recognized that some constraints are not changeable and the effect these can have on the group should be allowed for in the planning stage. It may well be that having regard to the constraints in existence, the operational aim of the group will have to be modified as the original concept will clearly not be possible of achievement.

Designing a group

The idea of 'designing' a group may sound rather false to many people on the grounds that, while houses and cars are inanimate objects and therefore subject to a planning process, such could never apply to human beings! Let us for a moment consider the alternatives. If no planning is involved, then anyone can gather together a haphazard collection of people with no idea of what they or anyone else wants to do: no goal would be set and no method of doing anything would be advocated. Whatever the problems of the collection of people they would hardly be improved by this kind of approach.

However if such a collection were started and there was a basic bit of planning behind it, i.e. that the collection would try to sort out by discussion what resources they had between them which could be used to help the less fortunate members, then a very different picture would emerge.

Basically the design of any group must be concerned with purpose. Having decided to set up a group to meet some kind of situation, then all the factors which will help that group to achieve the operational end of dealing with that situation have to be considered. Some will be seen to be more beneficial than others and they will be given priority in the planning.

For instance having decided that the best way of introducing people to the problems of adoption is to get a group of parents interested in adoption to meet together with some parents who have already adopted children, and ask them to share their ideas and feelings about adoption, then certain factors assume greater importance than others. It becomes necessary to have a meeting room in which people cannot only feel relaxed but also in which they can move about fairly freely and talk to one another. The number of meetings will be set at a low number, say six, because the operational aim of the group, the exchange of information and feelings, will not take a great deal of time to be effected. The role of the group leader will be that of guide, information-giver, and gentle co-ordinator of the meetings.

Of course designing a group calls for a good knowledge of what different group set-ups can achieve and it is lack of this kind of knowledge which tends to make people throw a group together on the assumption that it will work out all right when everybody gets together. This haphazard approach may be successful but it is usually no credit to the leader if it is.

It is simple to say that people's needs are different and that therefore the ways in which they are met should match those differences. In essence this is what should be aimed for. In practice it is not always that easy to achieve.

A group was established in a prison for prisoners who were isolates. The planning for the group suggested a careful screening of the possible members; a group which was no more than seven or eight in size and one which was also closed. The original design suggested that the group should last six weeks, meeting on a weekly basis, and that the leadership would be directive — based on the fact that the members would need a great deal of security. Other design factors included the level of ability of the members to express themselves, similarity of intelligence levels, and stable social backgrounds.

Many factors were considered in designing this group, but one above all the others proved to have been wrongly assessed. This was the factor of time. In practice dealing with isolates takes far longer than six weeks at one meeting per week; six months would be a more reliable estimate.

When a group has been thought about, then the acts of

creating it entail a certain amount of responsibility. After all if the thought had not occurred, then the group would not have come into existence and by any standards this must mean some responsibility for seeing that the creation operates reasonably efficiently and without causing harm to anyone.

Some organizations recognize that the skill of the leader is a very important one and they tend to set up methods of training. Leaders created like this are usually referred to as 'designated' which only means that they are provided by some social agency and that they have some understanding of the processes involved. The title also serves to distinguish them from leaders who arise from within some already existing group structure and can thus be described as 'natural' leaders.

Neither of these categories actually defines the way in which the leader will operate. This is usually a matter of personal choice or dictated by the exigencies of the situation. For instance with a collection of people who know nothing about groups other than their own life experience, a leader may decide that until this group becomes more aware of what is involved, he will have to assume a directive role, that is to guide, to set tasks, and to develop the growing skills of his members.

It is not a good thing to think that people can be self-directing without some help in first recognizing what such a way of existing actually entails. Children like and need a sense of security which comes from understanding where they stand in relation to other significant people in their lives. The same is true of adults, especially those who for some reason or other have not developed or had the chance to develop effective social skills and coping mechanisms. This does not mean that such people should never be offered the opportunity to develop the ability to be self-sufficient. In fact quite the reverse is true. But the development should be allowed to conform to the needs of those involved and not be imposed as part of some philosophy which sees self-direction as a desirable end in itself without reference to the needs and abilities of group members.

A group leader then can act as a director; he can also act as a facilitator, an enabler or a resource person, or any one of several other roles. The main factor must be that the role he takes is appropriate to the situation of the group and of the abilities and experience of the members and also of the outcome the group has as its essential aim.

It is interesting to note that in America social work groups tend to be predominantly directive despite the social work credo which lays great emphasis upon the client in the social work situation being able to be self-determining. I think that the reason for this predominance is that directive groupwork is in a very straightforward sense easier and safer than more permissive forms. Why is this so?

Well one of the main problems that anyone wishing to work with groups has to face is that he is always going to be out-numbered by the group members. In a very real sense this poses a threat. This is usually met by the group leader assuming and hanging on to the control of the group so that he has the safety of being able to minimize the threat implicit in the numbers. This kind of self-defence shows up very clearly in all beginners in groupwork and has the effect of making the leader that much less sensitive to the other members of the group in that he is devoting so much energy to protecting himself that he has little left to devote to the needs of others. It also sets a role model for the rest of the group who, seeing the person who is supposedly knowledgeable about groups obviously protecting himself, immediately set about following suit and protecting themselves.

The concept of the role model is very important in group leadership. Without question telling people that they should behave in a particular way is one of the least effective ways of getting them to behave in that way. If people can see that they stand to gain either in prestige or to increase their satisfactions in some way, then they will be prepared to make the changes in their behaviour which will facilitate those required behaviours. If they can be shown that the behaviour in question actually brings about desirable results, then again there will be a strong incentive to adopt the behaviour demonstrated.

Now the position of the leader in many groups is one of power. By this I mean that he is seen to be a person of power by the other members. Whether he actually possesses power in his own view of the situation or not is irrelevant. Therefore what the leader does is usually very significant in setting the behaviour patterns for all the others. For example if the leader is unable to behave in an honest and open way himself he will have great difficulty in getting any of his members to behave in open and honest ways.

On scores of occasions I have opened a group session by saying that the members should introduce themselves. This is a common piece of group behaviour. But the important thing is not that it is done but how it is done. If I start off the group by introducing myself, the style that I choose tends to be followed in almost precise terms by those who follow. Thus if I refer not to me as a person but to things I have done and the positions and other status things about me, then the rest of the group will follow suit.

It is as well to remember that the role-model setting is one of the most important tools that the group leader actually has and with which he can start to set the patterns of behaviour in his group. It cannot be stressed too often that in a group situation if the group leader sees as part of his brief that the members of the group shall come to know and recognize what is going on, then he has a responsibility to initiate a pattern of behaviour in the group which makes explicit by verbalizing. Many people see something happen in a group and they say nothing about it. The assumption is that if they have seen it, then everyone else has seen it also. Of course this is not true. Group members have to learn this just as they have to learn that there is a need to display their feelings and responses more in this situation than there is in real life outside the group. In this way members can become aware of the way in which their thinking and feeling compares with that of others in the group, and the sense of sharing begins to develop and the sense of trust which stems from this.

Members

Leaders have no value if there are no followers and the

important resource in any group is its membership. As well as being a resource the membership is also a constraint in that the abilities of the members dictate what the group can or cannot achieve. Put another way, as the artist works with paints or stone or materials which limit what he is able to achieve, so the group worker is working with people, who are the raw material involved. The difference lies very clearly in that the limits of materials are usually known in advance while the limits of people have never been very clearly defined. Indeed one of the benefits of working in a group may well be the development of potential hitherto unsuspected and at any rate very often unused.

One thing has to be recognized from the start, that is that human beings react, behave differently in the presence of others than they would in isolation.

The 'raw material' of any group is the mixture of leader and members, because the total potential, that is, the ultimate limitation of what the group can achieve resides mainly in this Gestalt. Outside factors obviously impose other limitations but what the group can achieve is largely dictated by the combined potential, abilities, experience, attitudes, and relationships of the members and the leader.

While the essence of this statement is absolutely true there is another factor which has to be taken into account and which I have tried to allow for in using the word 'potential'. Group members frequently find that the group experience encourages them to risk behaviour which previously they have either avoided, or not suspected lay within their ability. So the concept of development has to be considered.

Thus whatever the abilities of the members at the beginning of a group, there is the possibility that the group experience can enhance certain areas. Equally of course the group may have the effect of reducing the abilities in some areas and of changing the focus or nature of them. In short 'change' is a distinct possibility in whatever direction or areas it may occur.

Tom Lehrer, the American humourist, once said, 'Life is like a sewer, what you get out of it depends on what you put into it!'

Membership of a group is very much like that — the more each individual is prepared to put into the group the more in fact he will receive from the group. This is a very difficult lesson to learn for some people, largely because, for a variety of possible reasons, they cannot trust themselves to other people. We have seen earlier how dependent we are on others and on being accepted by those whose opinions and respect we value, and how this produces the fear of 'making a fool of oneself' which we feel reduces our acceptability in the eyes of others.

This fear operates to make people cautious — and under the circumstances of our society quite rightly so. It is interesting to watch a group of strangers cautiously testing each other out — making assessments based upon previous similar experiences. Some people are so 'closed off' that they cannot make any adjustments and are disappointed by most new experiences — their fear of appearing less acceptable than they would wish keeps them heavily defended.

Now this is a great shame for a number of reasons both for those so 'closed off' and for the others with whom they come in contact. First, it is a fact of group life that when some members hold back their commitment to the group, not only do they reduce what *they* get from the group but they also decrease what is possible for the others. This we must look at later in some detail in terms of the individual member's responsibility not just for himself and his learning but for everyone else in the group as well. Thus the attitudes of members are a very real constraint on what any group can achieve. Second, the 'contagion' effect of 'closed off' members tends to reduce the possibility of an increase in commitment by those who are rather timid and need strong examples to follow and much support in order to be able to feel freer and more committed. This concept of support brings us to a consideration of the status of members.

Scapegoat

I have talked about the way in which members of a group take on various operations which eventually seem to become their way of life within the group. Thus one member can always be relied upon to act as pacifier in any kind of row which develops, someone else keeps an eye on the time, another is a reliable spur to getting on with the job, and so on. Most of these roles are beneficial and there is no reason why they should not be exercised by others when they see or feel the necessity of behaving in this way. However, when a 'role' is ascribed to a member it usually means that he performs it with greater frequency than anyone else and that there is some expectation on the part of other members that he will act in this way. As long as he gains satisfaction and a sense of useful participation no doubt he will do so.

However some roles while equally frequent in their occurrence are of a different nature. One of these is the role of scapegoat. This biblically originating role is a frequent headache to groups and leaders and must be seen to have several important implications.

First, there are at least two major variants, temporary and permanent. But what kind of behaviour is common to both? In the Bible the scapegoat was the animal which was ritually laden with the sins of the village and then driven into the wilderness to die, thus cleansing the people of that particular load of sins. Over time the term has come to mean those who are blamed for not only their own faults but the faults of others as well. So we find in any community great or small individuals or groups who are blamed when things go wrong or even when there is a wish that things would go better.

In some senses such individuals and groups draw off much bad feeling, thus freeing the rest of the group to work more productively and harmoniously together. Of course those who are scapegoated in such a way may not feel that they are conferring any useful assistance on the society of which they are members.

All scapegoats, either in society at large or in small groups, tend to be picked for the role in two ways. First, they themselves expect that they will be treated badly by others and thus draw upon themselves the kind of behaviour they have learned to expect, so that their expectations become a self-fulfilling

71

prophecy. This is in reality a special case of the other major reason for scapegoating which is that those selected for this role are in some obvious way different from the others. The difference may not be a visible one, though these differences frequently are the basis of attention and form a link with other differences which may be more vital. The difference can be in any area of existence, speech, habits, attitudes, beliefs, and so on. Behaviour is often a significant point. Where one member of a group tends to respond in a way which is different from the others, he becomes the possible target for an action of scapegoating.

Thus temporary scapegoats occur when the 'difference' which becomes noticeable to the others is concerned with lagging behind, preventing the group from moving forward, using behaviour patterns which the group has rejected in favour of something else, and so on. In some senses behaviour like this undermines the security of the group by reminding them how new their current behaviour is, and some element of anxiety informs the dislike with which they tend to regard such behaviour. They hope by threat to re-create an 'all in the same boat' state which has strong elements of security about it. When the scapegoat's behaviour conforms, the scapegoating process tends to cease unless the person also happens to be a permanent scapegoat.

The obvious difference of some people seems to incur dislike and a position of permanent recrimination. Now it would appear logical that no person would be prepared to tolerate such a situation, but many do and we must assume that in some 'odd' way it provides them with satisfaction.

A young man whose behaviour was quite bizarre on occasions was every week made the centre of some fairly malicious horse-play and ridicule in a therapy group. He continued to attend with unfailing regularity and endured these sessions with good humour. Other members occasionally expressed concern, both at their own behaviour and at the victim's ability to take the ridicule. When he did not come one week they were very concerned and expressed concern lest he had been driven away and avowed that they missed him. When he returned, for a short period of time they made a fuss of him and then gradually reverted to their usual behaviour.

The man in this group gained more satisfaction from the ridicule of his fellow members than they could credit. He was an isolate, unemployed, and could spend whole days without conversing — the attention he received in the group was more than reward for the ridicule he also received. The group laid off its bad feelings on this one person and was able to work more freely as a result. The eventual outcome was that the group leader created other opportunities for contact for the scapegoat, withdrew him from the group and for a while accepted the role himself until the group developed other methods of coping with their bad feelings.

The permanent scapegoat then tends to be a person who is obviously different from the others but who is also of value to the group and whose level of satisfaction is being met by his membership. A very delicate balance is involved here and even willing sacrifices are not a very good example of leadership skill. No one person should be allowed to make such a sacrifice unless all involved are totally aware of what is involved and conscious choice is invoked.

It is as well to remember two things in this context:

1 People will tend to stay in situations when the level of satisfaction exceeds dissatisfaction or there are no perceived or available alternatives.
2 Satisfaction in this context is entirely personal and idiosyncratic, often apparently illogical and always concerned with so many factors that are unknown to others that it is always safer to speculate that it exists or that movement is possible than to suppose it does not when people make no move to change their position.

Central person

One of the roles which a leader can be seen to be occupying fairly frequently is described as that of 'central person'. If we think of the hub of a wheel, the focal point about which everything else revolves and more importantly to which everything is positionally related in a fixed order, then the centrality of the leader's role should be clear. It is an important concept for a whole variety of reasons, some of which we can discuss here.

If a group has been created by the operation of the leader first, seeing a need and then setting up the group, all the members will have been approached before the establishment of the group on a one-to-one basis by the leader in an attempt to put forward the value a group could have for that person. Thus when the group convenes for the first meeting as a group, the one relationship which all the potential members have in common will be that which they have established with the leader in his setting up procedures. Of course other common relationships may well exist depending on the nature of the selection of group members.

The common relationship is a key point. It cannot have escaped notice that groups tend to identify similarities and that in the early stages of the development of the group, similarities can be reassuring. People form clubs, select friends, and choose to work with others on the basis that similarity, complementarity, make life easier and more rewarding. One of the great advantages that groups have is that they offer the possibility of discovering that other people have the same or similar problems, produce similar responses, and are pleased to meet others in the same boat for the comfort it offers of not being too different, isolated, or compelled to struggle alone.

Much else can stem from the central person role of the leader and it behoves any person convening a group in this way to recognize that it creates the possibility of this kind of a perception of a relationship. Tied very closely to this may also be perceptions of power either allied to expertise or emotionally to a paternal figure. It cannot be stressed too often or too forcefully that such perceptions arise *whether the leader intended they should or not* and to deny their existence is to dispute the reality of the members and to belittle their perceptions as unworthy of

74

consideration. It is necessary to accept that perceptions will have occurred and to say so, to check out to what extent they have arisen, and how inimical if at all they are to the proposed development of the group.

Of course leadership responsibility is usually very high in the initial stages of a group, when some central power has to operate to set things up. This can all change later as things become more settled, but many promising groups have been either retarded or destroyed by the initiating leader's being too ready to hand over responsibility for the group's welfare long before it is ready or even wants to accept such a task. Thus the central-person gambit is custom built to generate exactly the kind of attitude which will allow the leader to exercise careful responsibility in the initial establishing period of the group's life.

Like all exercises of power it can be overdone and the scene may be set for domination by the leader. If this is what he sees as essential for the group's welfare, then this is a conscious choice, but if it occurs through insensitivity to the possibility, then a problem has been created for the time when change to a less directive approach may not only be desirable but essential for the group's health.

Of course if the original thesis was to set up a group which had a directive leadership, e.g. in an area of treatment with all the implications of superior knowledge being applied for the benefit of others, then the central person form of establishing a group gets the group off to the right kind of start.

One other possible form of this approach merits attention here. The power which the central person may be perceived as possessing is not at all or even necessarily always the same. Some paternalistic group leaders are seen as being essentially wise and understanding, others charismatic, some as possessing authority which has obviously been vested in them by a higher body, reputation, skill, personality, and so on.

Now there is a very strong need for any leader to recognize how he is perceived by his group members because, however ridiculous their view may seem to him, for them it is reality and all his actions and their responses will be interpreted in the light of it. Many times after working long hours with groups of people I have found them saying that it had taken them quite some time to get used to me as a person working with them and not what they had supposed me to be by reputation. I am always chagrined on these occasions that I have not had the wit to recognize these feelings earlier and to respond to them so that they can be adjusted to the reality of the situation. I might add that one reason for these incidents is that they occur among groups of people usually so competent and adjusted that it is very easy either to forget, or it seems ludicrous to suppose that such attitudes can exist.

The role of central person is unique and offers an opportunity for the leader to move fluently in any one of a number of major directions. Like everything else connected with groupwork the essential basis is recognition — seeing what has happened, being aware of it no matter how dotty it may appear to be. One of the commonest phrases I find myself using to people learning about groups is that they must 'blow their minds' — in other words widen the basis of their reception of behaviour and be prepared to accept what at first blush appears unusual as very probably correct.

The major factors covered in this chapter can be summed up as follows:

1 *Conceptualization* This covers getting the first idea — that a group could be a useful instrument. But it also covers consideration of many factors which will have or could have influence either in the creation or outcome of the proposed group. The concept of design has been stressed here largely because there is a strong need to counteract sloppy thinking in this area. The potential value of a group is so great that to fritter a lot of it away and also to risk frightening people away from group activities just through over-eagerness and thus not putting in enough thinking at this stage is a great waste. Of course it is a difficult exercise and of course many things will not be given enough consideration as will emerge later. But there is no

way in which a group leader can learn this part of his business except by attempting to do it as well as he can and keeping careful note of what he did and comparing it with what emerges as the group develops.

2 *Constraints* These factors influence outcomes — some can be changed others cannot. The major ability is to recognize how those in the second category are going to affect what the group will be able to do. Some constraints are very definitely facilitative, i.e. they help the group; the concept of constraint is meant to imply that at some point the factor will provide a boundary; boundaries can be supportive as well as restrictive. An illustration of the effect of constraints will be offered in the ongoing example at the end of this chapter but special consideration has to be given to (a) members and (b) the leader and his acts.

The characteristics, abilities, experience, attitudes, status, and relationships of the members are the basic resource and the major constraint of the group. The interaction is so important that on many occasions group leaders will attempt to use what knowledge they have of potential group members to select those whose attributes will add to the development of the group as a working instrument best designed to achieve its avowed ends. Of course such knowledge may only develop as the group proceeds and then the leader has two major directions in which he might go. First, he can use some form of re-selection using the knowledge he now has to regroup his members. Some groups, where the blend of people is important, may actually run selection sessions when potential members are observed in action and selection is made on the observed data and the mix of the eventual group guaranteed to be as effective as humanly possible.

In many groups such precautionary and logical steps are not feasible or even desirable. The second way is thus the path of accommodation and compromise. By this I mean that, recognizing what the inability to select for an appropriate mix entails, the leader will need to see clearly what he can achieve of his original goals with the mix he has got. Of course unrecognized potential will play just as an important part here as in the first way. Indeed what usually emerges is that starting from either point the actual outcome is usually somewhere different because of factors not allowed for. This does not invalidate either of the points of departure but only serves to add a realistic dimension.

Leaders of course are a constraint in the sense that the way in which they conceptualize, create, and operate the group has already pre-empted some of the options. Naturally whenever a choice is available, one eliminates the factors not chosen for the time being. Obviously the characteristics, abilities etc. of the leader are just as much potential and constraint for the group as are those of the members.

It must be recognized that the whole area of conceptualization, design, and thinking-through are leadership acts in that if they are not taken, nothing will be eventually created. Much more will be made of other leadership acts in later chapters.

An example

It seemed to me that one of the best ways in which I could demonstrate some of the points I am trying to make would be to offer an analysis of a group situation in the hope that it would show clearly the step by step processes involved. I have chosen to use the example of a group of social work students for a whole variety of reasons. First, it takes the idea of group activity out of the field of therapy where it has all too often reposed and placed it in the field of learning which is much more appropriate for the kind of group work discussed in this book. Second, it shows very clearly many of the constraints which affect the groupworker in general, e.g. a pre-selected group, clearly defined time limits, and breaks in contact. Third, it emphasizes many of the good points of groupwork, e.g. clarity of purpose, the application of leadership, the developmental stages of a group, and so on.

The various stages of the group are described as part of chapters 4-8, each stage being that which is relevant to that particular chapter.

Stage one Conceptualization I have always maintained that there is no real substitute for group experience. If one is going to learn how to work with people in a group, then it becomes essential that experience within a group is one of the major factors of preparation. It stands to reason that if the major skills of a group worker are of a practical nature, then theoretical knowledge is a point of departure and not the main point of arrival.

This being so I have always tried to give students who were learning about groups the opportunity to work in groups and to use these work groups as instruments of learning about groups in general. Where a group of students is large this poses some difficulty, but where it is of the order of 9-15 the solution lies in regarding the total number as the population of the group.

Let us now look at the logical sequence which follows.

1 A small number of students have been selected to pursue a one-year course in social work.
2 Part of the course entails learning *about* groups and how to work with groups.
3 The need is to find the most effective way of achieving the maximum learning, given the constraints of time, other demands, the environment, the potential of the group members, resources etc.

Within the teaching system a group experience lasting over three terms is feasible. The theoretical inputs come from other sections of the course in part, partly from previous education and partly from being offered as the group sees some necessity for particular pieces of knowledge to cope with situations in which they find themselves. Within the learning situation the group experience is compatible with ethical and philosophical ideals of social work practice and will hopefully demonstrate the effects of offering this kind of learning to people and the need for absolute sincerity in pursuing a course of action like this.

The responsibility for establishing the group lies clearly with me as teacher and the general aims are reasonably well thought out and ready for presentation to the students so that a primary contract can be made.

It now remains to look at the possible constraints to see how they could affect the outcomes, to evaluate past attempts at this kind of learning to see what lessons could be applied to the current set-up.

The constraints Environment. This is generally conducive to this kind of learning except for the fact that the course norm of assessment produces particular difficulties and makes the development of trust between me as leader and the students as group members somewhat more difficult than would otherwise be the case. There is some expectation on their part that learning will be purveyed ... part of the ethos of a 'teaching' institution.

Time. There are three main factors here:

1 The duration of sessions and the necessity of fitting in with a timetable.
2 The frequency of sessions.
3 The amount of time when students are available, e.g. the limiting factors of the length of term, placement, and holiday time.

Resources. Rooms and equipment are little problem; the skills available should be adequate!

Members. Problems arise here because the members are selected on criteria not entirely compatible with those that would normally be used to choose people for a specific groupwork course, e.g. the interest of the potential members is in social work in general and any expressed interest in the use of groups in that field of endeavour is a bonus. This will pose some problems in terms of commitment. The learning potential is however high, previous experience shows some similarities, educational backgrounds are also similar, attitudes may be widely disparate but in general the potential is good.

Size. This at nine students is well within the reasonable limits of a learning group. This fact alone will be valuable as they will tend to work together as a group not only during groupwork sessions, but for most of their academic stint.

Open/closed nature of the group. This group will be closed as no new students will be added to the course once it gets under way. Of course this will tend to generate a more intense interaction.

Selection. This has already taken place based upon criteria of acceptability for social work training which are not necessarily the criteria for acceptance as students of groupwork.

Activity. This will be mainly some form of open discussion with comment but does not exclude the possibility of role-play, games, and exercises.

Intervention. Initially this will be directive but will become facilitative later. The main purpose is to inspire the ability to observe and understand the processes which occur in groups.

Contract. This will be initially based upon learning *about* groups. The major clauses of the primary contract will be left to the decision of the group as a whole within the overall constraint of the learning focus of the course.

For those who find this conceptualization somewhat too specific I would recommend looking at the article listed below.[2]

2 John Hodge, 'Social Groupwork — rules for establishing the group', *Social Work Today*, vol.8, no.17, 1 February 1977, pp.8-11.

5 Created for a purpose: from thought to action

Having conceived the idea that a group may be an appropriate way of dealing with a particular problem or situation, the next important piece of behaviour is to turn the thought into an action, i.e. to start and form the group. This is the area of greatest difficulty for the beginner. Many people have absorbed basic information about the way in which groups of people behave, but interestingly enough large numbers of these same people have never started groups. Is it because their interest was purely academic? Or are the usual excuses which are given true, e.g. that employers have never offered any encouragement or that there has never been enough time, opportunity, cash, resources etc?

Much more likely is the well-known difficulty of all professional training of turning what is learned as theory into actual practice. This problem is always enhanced by a lack of any opportunity to try out newly learned ideas under skilful and sympathetic guidance. Where such guidance is forthcoming the results are usually very startling in two ways. First, in the lack of apparently hard factual data which people who have had some training in the use of groups can actually have. The second lies in the success the same people can have when they are able to bring their problems to be discussed with group workers with a great deal of practical experience.

For example a group of probation officers set out to create different kinds of groups under guidance. Among these officers were several who were working as prison welfare officers and wanted to create groups within the prison. In any residential setting, as we shall see later, the constraints tend to operate with readily observable force. In a prison this is even more apparent. Thus one of the first pieces of learning that had to be made here was what was actually possible in the circumstances which obtained. It became obvious that if the discipline staff were not brought into the exercise right from the beginning and thus knew all about it, their lack of understanding about the group could quite easily sabotage it right from the start.

This only serves to highlight the fact that this kind of co-operation is required in whatever setting a group is to operate and may well be the first requisite of the establishment of a group

In chapter 2 we looked at the main ways in which groups originate. All of these origins showed that at some stage the process of thinking and exploring was turned into making contact with people, not only those who may well be directly involved as members but also all those who may have some ability to influence both the establishment of a group and its future life.

I have already hinted that people are an important environmental constraint. Let me give another example of how it operates.

A group of social workers in a large city area had decided that they would attempt to establish a group for children on the basis that it would form an intermediate treatment group. Now the concept of such a group, while partly accepted by the authority, had at that time never before been put into practice. When therefore the authority was asked to give its blessing to the proposed group, it hedged all its bets. The group could proceed but only on the condition (a) that it did not cost the authority anything (b) that it was not done during the time when the social workers were legally employed by the authority (c) that it was clearly recognized that there was no official underpinning for the project (d) that there would be no requests for reduced work loads in order to have time to work with the project and so on.

What might have had endless possibilities given minimal backing by the authority was hamstrung by lack of resources, tiredness on the part of the staff, and suspiciousness on the part of other agencies at the apparent lack of official backing. The effectiveness of the project was dependent largely upon the energy and goodwill of those involved, who incidentally were not given any help by being put in contact with those with experience who could have saved them a lot of time and trouble.

So the point must be made that the creation of a group takes place in an environment which affects the possible outcome of the group or even its viability. The degree of co-operation which is required from others in the organization or other agencies involved means that they not only need to know what is going on but also need to be convinced that their help is desirable. This requires active education on the part of prospective group leaders.

After the constraints have been considered the next step is to consider selection and contact.

The funnel

Selection of the members of a group has always been regarded as one of the ways in which a group leader can ensure that his group is effective. This implies the use of the 'funnel'. The funnel is so called because it is wide at the top and narrows down to the business end, which is precisely what the leader hopes to be able to do.

He starts with a fairly large number of people who would all stand to benefit by being included in the group he intends to run. This number may be twice even three times the number of places he sees as being available in the proposed group. The number will of course be arrived at on the basis of what is most efficient for the operational aim of the group, taking into consideration the constraints which exist and the potential of the members.

Through a process of interview and discussion with the individuals the leader will make choices based upon his aims for the group. He will thus gradually eliminate some potential members in favour of others. Eventually he will arrive at the narrow end of the funnel with the right number of members.

This is the classic selection process of the directive group leader. But most group leaders do not get the chance to be so choosey. Most of us are faced with a number of people either too small or too large for what we have worked out as the optimum number for the particular group we want to run. In many cases the group has already been selected on criteria which have little relevance for group development. For instance groups of students are selected for social work courses, not on the basis that they will be able to work together but on the fact that they satisfy the entrance criteria of the particular institution to which they have applied.

A pre-selected group then has to be considered as containing or subject to extra constraints and the effect these will have on the group's performance needs to be calculated very carefully. Some aims might now not be possible, others may have to be substituted.

Many examples of the problems of selection can be found in the literature of working with groups.

A number of students of a social work course spend part of their time in a group situation where the basic purpose is to use their observation of their own group to learn about the processes which are general to all groups. The students were selected for the course in the first instance not on their ability to work in groups but on criteria associated with being able to become good social workers. The kind of difficulties they experienced in learning to work together as a group was in no small measure due to the fact that the selection process had not created any immediately obvious bonds between them. So much of their time in the first few weeks of being in the group was devoted to discussing norms and standards and the structure of their group. This is a classic sign of anxiety among group members about their safety in the group situation. The development of a degree of trust over a period of time led to the dropping of this defensive tactic and cleared the way for the group really to get down to some productive work.

Some groups when working together to learn about skills in working with people have been selected on the basis of the job they already occupy. If they then decide to use a special form of group to enhance their learning situation, for example some form of sensitivity training, many factors may mitigate against such an exercise being a success. In the first instance many people will be there who do not want to indulge in this kind of exercise, having some fear of the outcomes. Even if ground rules are made in order to protect these people, the group is not likely to have a great deal of success because all the people involved were not really selected on the basis of being involved in sensitivity training. In any case the amount of time which should be devoted to this exercise is rarely available unless it has been planned for in the first instance.

Group workers often take over groups established for other purposes, e.g. gangs, families etc., where selection is not possible at all. These situations highlight clearly the need of the convenor to be as sure as is humanly possible of what it is he is trying to do, because only then will he be able to make a reliable estimate of how far the existing constraints will modify the desired outcome.

Clarity of purpose

It is essential that the purpose for which a group is created should be clear. At least as clear as it is possible to be, given the circumstances in which the convenor finds himself. The whole process of the establishment of any kind of group is intensely logical.

If the necessary thinking, discussion, preparation, and exploration have taken place, then the convenor is in the position of being able to present to the potential group members a proposition. It is unquestionably true that faced with stating this proposition and answering questions about the proposed group, gaps in preparation are readily exposed. The idea that people should share problems, skills, or knowledge is not one which is readily accepted in our society, except in certain clearly defined areas of everyday life like clubs and families — the concept may have to be sold. Co-operation for events, that is clearly defined, one-off experiences, is often much easier to come by and does not seem to contradict the generally accepted cultural precept that a person must stand on his own feet or be dependent only on acceptable (traditional) groups.

Whether a group leader takes over an existing group or attempts to create one by selecting individuals to comprise it, he is faced with the need to explain clearly what he is about and to obtain the consent of those involved at least to give it a try. In the discussion on 'central person' (chapter 4) it is shown that a particular kind of relationship can develop between leader and members as a result of this operation.

Very often the discussion about joining the group or about using an existing group for a new purpose, e.g. using the family group as a vehicle to examine its own processes, is referred to as primary or initial contract or as a working agreement. Before looking at this concept in more detail it is only necessary to say that this factor can be carried to great lengths. The fact is that it is based upon an approach to human beings which advocates that co-operation between people is best ensured by their understanding what is involved and by giving a voluntary commitment to be involved based on that understanding.

In many cases the first contractual obligation may just be that the individual approached will think about what is being offered and may then turn up at an initial meeting where future progress will be decided upon. Of course some people are requested to join groups as part of a contractual obligation already formed. For example a psychiatrist may use groups as part of his treatment plan and patients may be expected to join groups as part of their treatment programme, refusal may be deemed to constitute a breach of a medical contract already in existence.

Contract

A contract is a working agreement between the group leader and the members of the group. It has several very important functions, not least to register the varied expectations of the various parties to the group commitment.

When a collection of people gather together there well may be an assumption that all, being reasonably intelligent, will have roughly the same idea of why they are there. Usually nothing is further from the truth. Each and every person, however much publicity has been put out beforehand, will have only assimilated that part of it which relates to his previous understanding and ideas. This being so, the disparity of expectations will be quite great and, if not taken into account, will create the possibility of high levels of disappointment for many of the members.

How can a contract help with this problem? Quite simply by asking everyone to spell out what they think they are meeting in the group to do. This applies to children as well as adults, to those who are not supposed to have any ideas as well as to those who have too many.

Clearly from the group leader's point of view it places a burden on him to know exactly what it is that he has to offer. This means that he will have to have thought through the reasons for starting his group very clearly. He may still come up with the understanding that he is not absolutely sure of what he wants to achieve and this will then make one of the major points of his side of the contract. He will suggest that by working together they will be able to use the different skills and abilities to further the common end, rather than suggesting that he knows what is best and will guide everyone to the most effective achievement. If however he feels that he does know what is required, then he must say so quite clearly that this is what he is offering.

The prospective members will have their ideas about what they want out of the situation even if these are somewhat hazy. They must be encouraged to say what those ideas are because they will soon see that not everyone has similar ideas and a certain amount of bargaining will need to be entered into if enough areas of sufficient satisfaction are going to be covered for everyone.

A very important part of the operation of contract is that it should be flexible. No one can be sure how things are going to work out, though obviously the more experienced people will probably have a better idea of this than those who are experiencing their first group. Thus a contract which is rigidly maintained from the starting of a group is liable to be one which less and less fits the needs of the group.

At the beginning therefore it is advisable to indicate that the contract is modifiable as the group grows and changes. Any modifications are to be discussed and only to be effected if there is a general consensus. If the group exists in an environment in which very firm rules about behaviour exist, then the original contract will have stated this as one of the immovable constraints within which the group will need to proceed. In some cases no amount of consensus will be able to change the major constraints, but at least discussion of them will ensure that their influence is clearly rather than vaguely understood.

Apart from being a working tool of great value in ensuring a high level of satisfaction and member participation, contract clearly has a non-verbal contribution to make. It says that one of the main learning purposes of a group is to carry responsibility for one's own actions and not to be dependent upon others past the point where that dependence is either necessary or useful. The whole basic purpose of using groups, i.e. to help people use the resources they possess in conjunction with others is underlined by the contract. It is a clear statement of shared and co-operative endeavour.

All areas of the group's construction, running, purposes etc., can be subjected to contractual agreement. Thus the very mechanics of the group, what time it will start, how long sessions will last, the duration of the group, its nature, the kind of activities are all subject to contractual agreement within the reality of the constraints which exist.

A club had been formed by local authority social workers designed to be a place where people who had been inpatients of the local psychiatric hospital could meet once a week for social and recreational purposes. The contractual agreement made between the organizers and prospective members before they left hospital included also the suggestion that social work help would be available, but on request only. The club was therefore to be run by a committee and the social workers would operate as advisers and consultants if required. After a period of time during which the club ran very successfully, the contract was modified to include the provision of groups within the club structure which had a much more overt therapeutic nature as these were felt to be valuable by the club members.

The basic contractual obligations were discussed with the club as a whole and the conditions of provision of the groups drawn up. They became a successful feature of the club, but support for them and attendance varied as the club membership changed.

Activity choice

One of the major areas of contractual agreement lies in the area of what activity the club will pursue in order to achieve its ends. Often enough the very nature of the group clearly indicates what this will be, though not so often clearly seen is the fact that the main function of the group and the kind of activities which serve to establish and maintain it in existence are not necessarily even similar.

Thus the establishment of most groups takes organizational skill which involves propaganda, advertising, committee procedures, endless discussion, mediation, contact etc. The group when established, depending on its nature, may require skills of a different order connected with a knowledge of the dynamics of groups and the ways these can be harnessed to fulfil the group's aims. It is not always possible to discover the two rather different skills in one person; it may not even be desirable.

When people are asked what they think groups 'do', answers vary from one extreme, that of talking, discussing, decision-making, to what are usually lumped together as activities, that is games, leisure activities etc. Of course this is true, but it is unfortunate that in this country historically the use of created groups has tended to fall into the extremes of this continuum. Thus most people are familiar with the idea of groups for recreational and leisure purposes and perhaps less are familiar with groups used for so called 'serious' purposes like committees, decision-making bodies, and forms of 'treatment'.

Of course familiarity exists with the idea that children can play in a group, that young people may do quite a large number of their social activities in groups — it is a relatively startling idea that 'normal' adults might benefit from 'playing' in a group. My main points in making these comments are two:

1 The activity which is the main programme of the group can be selected from a wide spectrum of possibles. Its principle value must be only that it can obviously help to achieve what the group is aiming at, and
2 There is no valid reason why the activities performed by the group should necessarily remain the same throughout the life of the group.

If a group has been formed of young people who are either on the point of leaving or have left school, for the purpose of helping them to settle into the beginnings of adult life, then the group could discuss problems, successes, ways and means, and generally share what information they had. They could also be exposed to other sources of possibly useful information from expert or knowledgeable people. But there is no reason why such a group in fulfilling its function should not use other fundamental techniques.

Unusual situations cannot be well met just by discussing what is likely to happen. Much of the life of some young people is concerned with attempting to cope with situations for which they are not usually well prepared, e.g. job interviews, relationships with adults in work situations etc. All inventive people give their ideas a 'dummy' run if they can, in which scale models or prototypes of their ideas are tested for practicality in conditions which are simulated versions of the real thing. Groups frequently find this not only hilarious but also a very beneficial thing to do. Situations can be practised and although obviously 'artificial' in one sense, they can be productive of much social learning.

Inevitably the understanding about the ways in which other people might feel and behave in a given situation can be increased. Also there is the possible spin-off that learning about oneself will develop, because however 'artificial' the created situation may be, it is an interaction with 'real' people involved and therefore different and can be very illuminating.

With children and young people anyway the difficulty of getting them to talk about their lives is well known, especially if either long experience has made them bitter and suspicious or where their ability to verbalize emotions and less than concrete facts is not very high. This problem can frequently be overcome by providing an immediate experience, e.g. a game, an exercise, or some other kind of physically involving performance with other group members, which can then become the focus of discussion. Recency lends point to the discussion and it is not obviously connected with problem areas, though these will affect relationships and emerge in the discussion.

The technique sounds devious, but is essentially based upon two very important assumptions:

1 That the group members will gain some benefit from being able to talk about their problems or difficulties, and
2 That if a direct approach is inevitably going to be unsuccessful for many possible reasons, then bearing in mind the many ethical considerations involved and accepting that help is required, it must be valid to prepare people to receive help that they would otherwise reject for the wrong reasons, or at least reasons which are not valid, being based on ignorance or misunderstanding or conditioning etc.

So like most other factors connected with work with groups, the activities a group uses must be appropriate. Basically they should be adopted to achieve ends, empirically justified and within the ability of the group members to use. Of course great care needs to be taken in the choice of activities because different ones have different effects. Some activities separate individual from individual and need very careful handling in terms of integrating and sharing the individual experience. Nothing is calculated to use less of the dynamics of a group than activities which isolate and encapsulate the individuals so that although they may be occupying contiguous space, they are hardly aware of each other's presence and interaction between them is minimal.

I think enough has now been said to demonstrate that the activity choice is very wide and certainly includes the possibilities of co-operative work and group living, as we shall see later. The concept that a group was only a 'real' group when seriously discussing some fundamental problem of its members must be dispelled for one which indicates that there are many ways of using the dynamics of group interaction for the benefit of group members. Caution must be expressed however, lest the activity becomes the end rather than the means to an end. There are occasions when this is justifiable, in the use of the group to study its own mechanism for instance, but usually such an interest in activity tends to produce a stagnant group, as far as the productive use of group processes is concerned.

It is very difficult to write about operating a group from the point of view of the leader without creating the impression that leaders need to be omniscient. Of course this is incorrect, but I would also like to stress that our society has turned so much away from the concept of excellence in trying to improve the lot of some sections of the community that it is in fair danger of discrediting any kind of skill whatsoever as being a distinction of some sort. This may well be an exaggeration on my part but I offer it as a counter-balance, so that skill can be seen in its proper place in this context, that is, used to bring about circumstances which enhance the lives of all involved. In this context it is useful in the area of creating groups to look at the leader's responsibility in the 'rules of the game' and then to look at what have been called 'ground rules'.

Rules of the game

It may sound a little ludicrous to be talking about a 'game' and its rules when concerned with something as serious as working with groups. But it is one way of indicating the difference which is sometimes ignored which can exist between a group leader and other members of the group.

If a group leader is experienced and knowledgeable in the matter of running groups, then whenever he sets up a group he is in a position of advantage, as far as anything connected with a group is concerned, over the other members, unless some of those members are also experienced in working in groups. It is commonly assumed that because we all live and work in groups that we all understand the workings of groups equally well. But this is obviously not true. This is where the analogy with games comes in as a simple illustration.

It is almost impossible to play even the simplest of games with any degree of success if the rules which govern the game are unknown. This is the state in which most people enter a created group. In any game situation those who know the rules try to instruct learners so that they can start to play with some confidence, so that what they are doing is at least along the right lines. As they play longer they should become more adept and learn to use the rules with greater freedom, to be able to play creatively rather than just obediently. In other words they begin to be able to play for enjoyment rather than to learn.

The analogy with groupwork is close.

If new members of a group are to be able to derive maximum benefit from it, in the end then they will have to learn how to use the rules for their own ends. This means that the group leader in order to tap the resources of the group will have to teach it the rules of this particular game, and stand by to see that the rules are well and truly learned.

What are the rules of groupwork? Well they are the ways in which being a member of a group can influence the behaviour of individuals, the way power is given and used, the benefits which can be derived from the situation, and so on. In other words what the leader is trying to do is to teach the group members how to get the most out of the group of which they are a part.

Ground rules

The idea of 'ground rules' is somewhat similar to that of a basic contract, except that it is usually the leader who, from his wider experience and greater understanding, tries to limit certain possibilities. He may suggest for instance that one of the ground rules should be that if anyone is being very hard pressed by other group members, that member can appeal to the leader for help or even that the leader has the undisputed right to intevene to protect him.

In a very real sense these rules are limitations or boundaries placed upon the group by mutual agreement at its beginning. One major limitation involved is the age-old one of members agreeing to things which they do not clearly understand. But generally speaking what is concerned is a code of acceptable behaviour set up in advance. Such a code has a great chance of relieving the anxieties of some members of a group who may be aware of the stories about groups and may not be certain how far they want to be involved.

Two real values of ground rules are:

1 They can serve to speed up the process of getting on with the task by providing a protocol, and

2 They can provide a method of learning about a group before becoming too involved in it — a kind of foretaste or preview.

Against ground rules is the fact already mentioned of probable lack of understanding and allied to this the fact that agreement is rational and cannot really involve members at any true feeling level. It can therefore be an overt defensive device.

I give as an example below a set of ground rules quoted from Gendlin and Beebe (1968). The rules are established for a sensitivity training group and express quite clearly a particular belief about people and their development as well as about the way in which the group should function.

Ground rules for group sessions (Gendlin and Beebe, 1968)[1]

1 Everyone who is here belongs here just because he is here and for no other reason.

2 For each person what is true is determined by what is in him, what he directly feels and finds making sense in himself and the way he lives inside himself.

3 Our first purpose is to make contact with each other. Everything else we might want or need comes second.

4 We try to be as honest as possible and to express ourselves as we really are and really feel — just as much as we can.

5 We listen for the person inside, living and feeling.

6 We listen to everyone.

7 The group leader is responsible for two things only; he protects the belonging of every member, and he protects their being heard if this is getting lost.

8 Realism: if we know things are a certain way, we do not pretend they are not that way.

9 What we say here is 'confidential'; no one will repeat

1 E.T. Gendlin and J. Beebe, 'An experiential approach to group therapy, *Journal of Research and Development in Education* vol.1, 1968, pp.19-29.

anything said here outside the group, unless it concerns only himself. This applies not just to obviously private things, but to everything. After all, if the individual concerned wants others to know something, he can always tell them himself.

10 Decisions made by the group need everyone taking part in some way.

11 New members become members because they walk in and remain. Whoever is here belongs.

It is interesting to note that although these rules are designed for a special kind of group in many ways they are universally applicable, e.g. in terms of the confidential nature of the group's communication; of the need for all members to co-operate in the making of decisions; of the need to establish contact before any work can be done, and so on.

Little has been said so far about psychological and sociological concepts of the way human beings behave in groups or yet about the way such conceptions may be used to attempt to understand such behaviour. There are many reasons for this. One is that theoretical understanding of human behaviour, by which I mean that a constructed and consistent theory of behaviour is used as a yardstick to measure actual behaviour, produces either behaviour which is interpreted selectively so that it fits the tenets of the theory or wide generalizations or understanding of so detailed a portion that it is almost valueless. Clearly I do not mean totally valueless but of little value for the practical issues which face anyone working with a group of people.

What is essential are practical data which are sufficiently specific to be useful and general enough to have common application. That is we need what has been given the grandiose name of 'practice theory', a collection of principles, precepts, and empirical data about group behaviour.

However such practice theory has of itself no direction. For example the fact that a group leader knows that to increase the number of members in his group has certain effects, like increasing the ideas available and decreasing the time in which each member has to express them, does not give him any directive as to when or why such a manoeuvre should be undertaken. Two other factors at least have to be considered, the first being what the group is trying to achieve and the second the yardstick which the leader has against which he compares what he sees.

Of course right from the beginning any potential group leader must have some idea that a group can be used as a method to attain some end or he would never contemplate starting one. Thus such a leader is liable to have seen, heard, been in or otherwise known about, some form of group or to have received some information about groups from some source. All of us also have some criteria for the interpretation and understanding of the behaviour of others that we encounter every day. These criteria may be explicit or almost totally hidden according to our interests and experience, but in particular the amount of thinking we may have directed to the problem.

Given that a group is then created, the kind of leadership which will be involved can range from a basic precept like 'people are basically friendly and if left alone will soon learn to work together' to a very detailed and precise theoretical formulation of human behaviour like psycho-dynamic theory. I do not mean precise here in the sense of accurate but in terms of the minutiae of the theory.

In another sense then the possession of some concepts about human behaviour dictates the techniques which are used in the running of the group. The two major issues in this field have already been discussed in terms of whether the leader believes that he possesses most of the skills, knowledge and understanding and his members little or none, or whether he believes that the major resources lie in the group and his business is to create the opportunity for their use.

Let us take a very simple example of this. Given that the purpose of a group is to exchange information, then the relevant knowledge and skill in a group leader should be concerned with the ways in which people absorb different kinds of information and with the ways in which such absorption can be facilitated.

Thus if, as is commonly believed, people absorb information by having it presented to them clearly and efficiently, there is no problem. But the common belief is demonstrably untrue, especially when the information is either complex, unrelated to previous knowledge, or involves strong emotions. Other factors which are also involved are the relationships between the parties (e.g. teachers have long known that if they are liked by children that the children are willing to work much harder for them than for teachers they do not like) the environment, the degree of concentration possible, state of mind and of health.

Given that 'formed' groups can exert a strong conformity influence upon their members, then starting from different theoretical orientations this fact can be used in a variety of ways. Behaviourists use it to ensure maximum effort on the part of the individuals in performing the tasks which are part of the group programme. For instance rewards for successful achievements may be withheld for the entire group or some selected part of it until all members have completed their assignments to a given level. The pressure the group then exerts upon the slower and less accomplished can be quite great and may need monitoring. Of course the individual who has a score to settle with his colleagues can use this situation to withhold just rewards providing he can tolerate the pressure.

The pressure may hopefully be supportive rather than punitive and thus the individual can see what his accomplishments can achieve not only for himself but also for his colleagues.

An example

Stage two Creation This section of the example is devoted to describing how the learning group conceptualized at the end of the last chapter was brought into being.

The major problem is of course that the group as a collection of individuals already existed. So the creation of this group was really the formation of a unit from a general collection of people. Time is of the essence in this operation as it is no way possible to force people to recognize that they need to trust one another; the realization has to grow 'organically' with the recognition of what is and is not possible with the different levels of relationship.

The first task was to explain what we were about from my point of view, being the person with the most comprehensive overall view and experience. Then the students could say what they felt about the situation, recognizing two very important factors. These were their limited understanding of the situation and the restraints that the environment and the unfamiliarity would impose upon their freedom to express themselves clearly. The element of uncertainty is always a major factor in the first few sessions of any group which contains people whose experience of group life is very limited. I don't doubt from my own experience that it also applies to people with lots of time spent in groups.

From these first explorations the possibility of a primary contract emerges, that is I put as clearly as I can what I can offer the group and what I expect from it, and this can be aligned with what the students feel they can offer and what they want from it. No really irreconcilable desires emerged and we were able to form the basic contract on those areas of mutual agreement. In this particular group of students there was a strong need to proceed slowly from the kind of learning they were used to as postgraduates to the more experiential form which I believe is the most effective for learning about groups.

So our basic contract was information first and then after a period of about four weeks to review the situation and to plan the next move. This is well in accordance with the basic principles of contract-making in that the element of change was built in and based upon increasing knowledge and understanding with a consequent increase in the level of trust.

The students had to find out for themselves that the information they would receive could only be partly related to their previous learning and experience and that therefore some large part of it would not be of direct value. However as the contract was formed it enabled us to proceed and to start to work together. The relationship of the group members at this stage was that of individuals to one central figure and the level of suspicion was fairly high. This was shown in the way that comments were interpreted as being devious and manipulative and explanations of behaviour were constantly being demanded. Much later in the group's life it was very interesting to hear what members' feelings had been about this particular phase, and it is this kind of recall which allows a group leader to get an enormous insight into the problems of starting a group which are never very clear to him in the times when they are actually occurring.

This is the time when testing-out occurs and everyone in the group is trying to establish a sense of the other members, without sacrificing too much of their own security in the process. The relationships which already existed between various members of the group before coming on the course were much used during this period and had to stand a great deal of strain. Because most of the students were married and had family and other responsibilities there were strong motives for not remaining in each other's company longer than was absolutely necessary. This also delayed the formation of higher levels of trust and as we shall see later had to be dealt with by the group themselves when they recognized what this pressure was doing to their unity.

By the end of the period stipulated as input by the primary contract the group requested three things very close together. First, that a more experiential form of learning should replace the input sessions, second, that more time should be devoted to the sessions, and third, that they should be held in a room which was much more conducive of closeness than a lecture room. The basic contract was modified accordingly, the requests acceded to, and the group had begun to grow together with the beginning of realization of what group pressures were all about.

6 Three steps to success

Having set up a group then the next issue is how is it going to be run. This really is a matter of the ways in which a group leader uses his understanding of what goes on in groups in order to influence the group in one way or another, even if this influence can be seen as no influence at all.

This chapter is called 'three steps to success' for the simple reason that I think the three steps which will be outlined here are absolutely crucial to running a group effectively. The three steps are (1) The ability to observe (2) the ability to make appropriate interventions, and (3) the ability to assess the group's situation.

The ability to observe

Our society does not put a premium upon the ability to see what is going on under our very noses. The trouble which has arisen about identity parades, mistaken identifications which have cost people their liberty, and the use that TV can make of the inability of people to actually see what is going on, are all typical examples. We see what is sufficient for our daily routines and only when encouraged and when we have the time to relax and stare do we realize how much else is actually going on that we do not normally notice.

Now the ability to observe is actually very important in working in groups. Why? Well in an interview situation we may have one person to keep tabs on and this becomes fairly easy because our attention is not divided and we do not have to make decisions about which person we should be looking at. In a group exactly the reverse occurs. There are several people, not just one; they are all part of the unit of the group and they are all able to influence what it is going to do. Thus it is necessary to keep some kind of oversight of everyone.

The difficulty becomes obvious when one tries to put this simple and true fact of group life into operation. I find myself saying to potential group workers: 'Do not concentrate on the person who is talking at least not all the time. If you would see the effect that speaker is having on the others present, then you must look at them'. It is difficult. We are conditioned to look at the person who is speaking so that we do not miss the non-verbal cues which he is giving which add so much more meaning to what is being said.

Now if this is true about the immediate behaviour of individuals, how much more difficult will it be to look at the larger effect their behaviour is having upon the way the group is going?

In a group of ex-psychiatric patients who met regularly once a week for support in the business of readjusting to life, there were two who had said very little despite all the encouragement that the group leader, a social worker, could give. Then one week both people had something to say and the group worker encouraged them to say it. The dialogue went on for a long time and eventually the group broke up with hardly anyone else having said anything at all.
The following week before the group started the group worker

was reminded by at least two of the other members that they also were part of the group and pleased though they had been to see the two quiet ones begin to contribute they did not want to sit and listen to them all evening.

The larger effect of the two quiet ones had escaped the worker in his enthusiasm to encourage participation. If he had been monitoring the interaction of the group as a whole, he would have seen that in fact it had decreased, and that this had significantly reduced the level of satisfaction of the other members. Of course it could be argued that they had a responsibility to break up the dialogue themselves, but perhaps they had not reached the level of confidence or trust in the group which would have enabled them to take the risk.

It is not an exaggeration to say that good observation lies at the bottom of all successful work with groups. Most of us look at things but what do we see? We see what we expect to see, what we have learnt we are likely to see under the conditions which prevail. This means in fact that if we are going to be able to see what takes place in a group session, then we are going to have to tell ourselves many times that the conditions under which we are operating are not normal, and to learn to cope with an expanded reality. To contravene the convention of not being seen to watch people, to concentrate our attention outside ourselves, to watch what is being *done*, and to try to estimate the effect it will have on the group are all ways in which this new learning can begin.

In order to help this process it becomes necessary to look in greater detail at the distinctions of content and process.

Content and process

In the observation of what goes on in a group there are many areas of our past experience and conditioning which we have to overcome. This is because the past behaviour would in some way obstruct our vision of what it is essential to see clearly.

Nowhere is this more evident than in the need to emphasize process rather than content. Here we are again faced with the use of words which adds to the confusion. We have already looked at the group 'processes' (in the plural) and now we are talking about group 'process' (in the singular).

Everyone knows what a process is, but it is still very difficult to describe simply. A process is that which is going on ... it involves change, it is dynamic. The application of heat to uncooked food is the 'process' of cooking ... it changes basic materials from one form to another.

In a group, process likewise changes basic raw materials, that is the individuals (if the group is successful), by welding them over a period of time into a functioning unit. This is simple enough, but all large processes seem to be almost endlessly composed of smaller processes which contribute to the larger effect. Thus the overall process of the group is enabled by a series of smaller processes which take place, such as interaction between members and the development of acceptable ways of behaving in this particular group situation.

On the other hand content is not what the group is doing but what it is saying, and here we come upon a first-class snag. Our society is verbally oriented. That is we put a great deal of investment into the words we use. Any kind of spoken words seem to have a fascination and we have a well developed but erroneous belief that by using them in the 'right' way we can explain everything. Many people become very exasperated when others do not readily understand when words are spoken clearly and with evident import. The problems inherent in this kind of communication are dealt with elsewhere in this book. Here I am only concerned with the fascination of verbal expression.

When a group is talking, that is, people are speaking and being responded to, we tend to listen to the words. No doubt we also pick up a large number of the non-verbal clues like expression, gesture, tone of voice etc. But they are reinforcers of the message. However at the same time many other things are going on. For instance members of the group are observing rules of behaviour, they are expressing preferences, they are consolidating role and status, they are selling themselves as good people, powerful or weak people etc. In other words all the things referred to earlier as group processes are taking place and they all have as common currency exchange the words which are being used.

One of the major problems of anyone wishing to work with groups is now clear. Language ... words fascinate ... but if we pay total attention to the intended meaning of those words, the processes of which they are part, the behaviour and interrelation patterns will tend to pass by unnoticed. If we need to know what the group is *doing* rather than what individual members of it are saying, then we will have lost out.

Such is the fascination of our verbal exchanges that when one person speaks in a group, most people will look at the speaker, seeking non-verbal clues which will aid them in the understanding of what he is saying. If we would understand group processes, then we should pay less attention to the speaker and much more to everyone else. The reactions of the others will demonstrate what is happening in the group and that is the primary goal of understanding of anyone who would work with groups.

Accurate and effective observation depends upon the kind of checking the leader is prepared to do. Elsewhere in this book reference has been made to the fact that if assumptions are not checked out, then the possibility that the actions we will base upon those assumptions being at best only partially correct, increases.

Thus the leader who thinks that his group is not working and in fact is resisting the idea of working can take action on that thought if he wishes. However he would be well advised to check with the group if his perception of their behaviour squares with theirs. It is quite shattering on occasions like this to find that the bases for the thought exist almost exclusively within oneself and bear little reference to what the other members of the group are feeling. Of course there are many times when one's feelings and perceptions are an accurate reflection of what the rest of the group is feeling also. It is gratifying to realize that the latter situation tends to become more prevalent after a great deal of time spent with groups, when experience begins to count.

Co-leaders have many uses and reference to them will be made in different parts of this book. One main use is in giving feedback to the leader about his performance and another is in placing a second observation against the leader's so that some kind of check can be made. While engrossed in the actual management of the group, a leader may miss several of the interactions which are going on. A co-leader who is free of the control function can more easily devote his attention to such matters and, if he can then convey what he has seen to the leader, much can be gained in the way of a global picture of the group's activities.

Agreement about what each is going to handle is an essential in the co-leader set-up. Two people who are used to working in this situation can be seen to operate as smoothly and as efficiently as a well-oiled machine. Much depends also upon the kind of discussion which takes place after each group session so that the leaders begin to get a clear picture of the ways in which they can help and support each other for the benefit of the group.

The mystic circle

When groups are used to exchange ideas and to talk freely with one another, then the formation of the circle is nearly always used and this has come to have some significance beyond its essential value. It has been said to represent democracy and equality in that a circle has no definite head or tail and thus the leader is seen to be equal to the other members and they to him.

Of course there is an element of truth in this, but the main reason for sitting in a circle is a much more practical one. If the members of a small group are going to interact freely with one another, then they need to be able to see one another without an undue amount of changing of positions every time they want to say something or to be able to see the expression on someone's face when they are saying something. Quite simply the human range of vision is very restricted. Our eyes are designed to see what is directly in front of us clearly and things that are to the side less clearly unless we turn our heads. The sixty-degree angle of clear vision with the head held rigid is called the cone of vision and only large objects and movements are visible to each side of it.

Sitting in a circle then makes the absolute most of this 'cone of vision' and allows people to be aware of all the others within the group with the minimum of head movements. There is thus nothing particularly mysterious about the circle. No doubt the sense of democratic equality plays a part in this situation, but I am only too well aware that a very dominant personality can make his presence felt and control the proceedings equally well in a circle as in any other formation of a group.

The converse of being able to see everyone else is of course that everyone can see you and this makes it very difficult to hide in such a group formation. However people will draw back from the circle and they will also lean forward. Both states may mean something or nothing very much according to the circumstances in which they occur. But when people are eager to contribute they will tend to lean forward to emphasize their points or to agree with another member. Also when they are bored or little interested they will tend to lean back out of the proceedings.

Another point which can probably be made here is the kind of attention that some group leaders pay to the positions that members take up within the circle. Now this is all very well, providing that the members have had the opportunity to choose the seat they occupy for themselves. Thus if each session of a group starts socially in one room and then the members move into another for the group session and are able to take their seats when all are present, then some attention can be directed to the possible indications that choosing one seat rather than another may have.

One well-known aspect of this is the oft-repeated idea that the person who sits directly opposite the leader is a potential challenge to him. Once again there is a very simple explanation of how this came about. In repose the head tends to assume a forward looking position as this is most comfortable for the neck muscles. In this position the eyes tend to be looking straight forward, i.e. they are looking directly at what is opposite. It is obvious that any leader cannot keep his eyes in constant movement around the group and that by sheer habit the number of times that he is looking straight forward must be significantly larger than when he is looking somewhere else. The net result of this may well be that the person sitting directly opposite begins to feel that he is either under more direct scrutiny than anyone else or that he is being offered more cues to contribute to the discussion. Either way he is liable to feel mildly threatened and to respond by making a larger contribution than he would normally have done, verbally or non-verbally. It must be admitted however that when a member knows this about the position opposite the leader and still deliberately chooses it, then there are some grounds for thinking that he may be making a challenge to the leader's position.

Feedback

Nicholas Greenwood writing in the *Guardian* in February 1977 suggested that it was difficult for schools to get some real idea of what the parents of the children felt about what was going on in the school. Parent representatives could hardly spare the time to go round all the people they represented and ask them for their views. In any case those views would tend to be so diverse that true representation of them would hardly be possible for one person. Greenwood goes on to say that if school managers could form 'working groups' of parents and teachers separate from the managing body, they could discuss and submit reports on the school's major proposals. Here teachers would get an opportunity to articulate their ideas and to talk about their practice while children's parents could fill in the gaps from their view of the school's business and their own feelings about what they felt they required for their children.

Of course there is very little that is new about a suggestion like this. It has been chosen for two main reasons. First, it uses the concept of a group rather than individual consultation. Second, it introduces in a familiar form the concept of 'feedback'.

The group use is an obvious one in that if an exchange of ideas is required, then the people who are going to do the exchanging need to be in a face-to-face situation. Moreover such a group would serve to demolish stereotypes, to personalize the people involved one to another, and above all to give them the important sense of being involved in the decision-making process, which as we have seen is fundamental in creating a high level of satisfaction for members of groups.

However our prime purpose is to study the effects of feedback and in order to do this we have to introduce the idea of assumptions. Every day of our lives we make assumptions about the reasons for other people's behaviour. Where such behaviour tends to fit into the normal patterns that we expect, then the basic assumption that we make is that all is going as usual. Where behaviour becomes in our view somewhat odd then we try to work out what sort of reason could possibly account for it. Thus if someone has treated us rather coldly, we may say that they appeared to be preoccupied and did not therefore notice us. We would probably not be too offended by this. If however we thought that the behaviour was a deliberate affront then our reaction would be very different according to the circumstances.

Now if human beings were as logical as they like to think they are, then this situation need not arise. The basic assumption about the piece of behaviour was that it was deliberate and therefore insulting. Logically if any element of doubt exists, the obvious thing to do would be to check whether the assumption was correct before acting upon it. Of course very few people do this for the simple reason that the feelings engendered by the supposed affront are sufficient to promote retaliation rather than a request for enlightenment.

This kind of response sours many individual relationships and is the cause of much unhappiness and misunderstanding. In itself this is bad enough but when it comes to large organizations which behave in the same way, then the damage can be increased many fold. This is where the concept of feedback comes in.

Feedback is a term borrowed from engineering where self-regulating mechanisms have been in use for a very long time.

110

Consider the safety valve on a steam engine. When the pressure of the steam reaches a predetermined level which is regarded as no longer efficiently safe, it causes a valve to open which allows the steam to escape until the pressure is reduced to a 'safe' level when the valve closes. If this principle is applied to human behaviour, then warning has to be given that certain things which are being done at the moment are passing the zone of safety. In other words they are going to cause danger, conflict which is unnecessary, or some other form of hurt. The assumptions which have been made that everything was fine need to be checked out. Feedback implies that if you make an assumption about behaviour or organization which is in fact wrong, then there may be no way of your knowing this to be so if you do not check it with the other people concerned. Assumptions do not matter all that much if no action is to be taken upon them. But action taken upon wrong assumptions, even if made with the best will in the world, can only be as wrong as the assumptions upon which they were based.

In the illustration offered the school and the parents would be in a position to get feedback from each other, and any assumptions that they had made about the behaviour or the plans or ideas of the other would be subjected to scrutiny; they would be brought out into the open and thus assumptions would have to be checked against what was seen there.

Feedback is not only important in group situations but in all aspects of human relationships, especially where behaviour which can and does affect the lives of others is going to be based on it. Clearly it is also one very important way in which we can continuingly check on our own self images by monitoring the feedback we get from others about the way in which they see us behaving as opposed to the way we think we are behaving.

In operating groups it is necessary constantly to monitor the responses of members in order to assure oneself that what is going on is what one has thought was going on. This often takes the form of a direct statement of the nature of 'What I see happening is that the group appears to be getting away from the basic task'. Note that this is a statement of one person's assumption. It is not a statement of absolute fact which would have had the form 'What is going on is the group is not getting on with the task', or words to that effect.

The first statement is unchallengeable because it is a statement of what one person thinks he sees. Other people may see something different and the form of the statement leaves every opportunity for them either to agree or disagree in the sense that their impression of what is going on is either similar or dissimilar. The second statement on the other hand, because it appears to be absolute, is challengeable. It may be regarded as an authoritative remark by someone who possesses a great deal of power in which case it may be resented but remain unchallenged.

The first statement is a request for confirmation that the way that the person who made it sees the situation is the way it is for all or most of the others. It is asking for feedback, feedback which is necessary in order that actions taken are based upon the situation as it is and not upon some exclusively biased view of it, feedback which is in action a self-reviewing mechanism which allows any organization to take an overall view of what is happening and thus make more effective decisions.

The ability to make appropriate interventions

Of course the ability to intervene in a group is totally dependent upon the observation that has been made of what the group is doing and of what its needs are at that time. A computer is only as good as the information it receives and this is even more staggeringly true about intervention in human situations.

We have seen something of the many ways in which a leader in a group can operate, but basically they are all covered by the fact that no intervention of any kind is necessary if the group is pursuing its way to its goals with all the skill at its command. Intervention by anyone, leader or not, can be justified in the first instance on only two grounds. The first of these being personal, i.e. to save oneself from some real or perceived danger and second, to move the group more in line with achieving the goal which it has set for itself. Now in the situation of

112

the leader of a newly formed group there will be little ability on the part of most of the other members either to see what is needed or to be able to know what to do about it even if they are perceptive enough to know that something needs to be done. Thus the responsibility falls upon the leader to make the moves which are necessary. This redresses what was going awry, but more than that if it has been done with skill, it will have done something else. It will have shown members the way in which some intervention in the future can be made by them. This means that the original intervention must be made without making it appear that only can such a thing be achieved if there is an enormous amount of skill and experience to back it up. Of course if the group leader wants his group to be dependent upon his skill and knowledge all the time, then he need not make this concession for it is not part of his contract to increase the group skills of the members of his group.

Intervention must have a focus. That is it must be used in an area of group behaviour which is important to either the survival of the group or its achievement. A great deal will be said about this aspect in the next chapter. To be able to be focused means that the group leader must be clearly aware of the purposes of the group and also equally clear about whether what is going on at the moment is leading towards or away from those purposes.

> This was the critical stage when the group could have disintegrated. There was also the danger of the angry minder being scapegoated. We, as leaders, had to try and steer a middle course, acknowledging the anger, but at the same time supporting the more positive aspects of the job that people had started to recount. We dealt with the angry minder by drawing out the very warm feelings she had for the children she looked after, so getting sympathy for her from the group and at the same time drawing out other members' warm feelings.[1]

It is significant that the intervention recorded here not only

1   Angela Simmons, 'Helping minders help themselves ...', *Community Care*, 1 January 1975, pp.22-3.

dealt with the immediate needs of the angry member but also was concerned with the survival of the total group. The author points out that after this incident the leaders were much more relaxed and confident of success for the group.

Initiation ceremonies

The illustration below is taken from the activities of a group of psychiatric patients discharged from treatment, who had been meeting as a group for several months. The leader of the group was a social worker and during the existence of the group no new member had been added. The illustration is a good example not only of an initiation ceremony but also of the problems facing a newcomer to an established group and of the expectations that people have of situations.

> At the request of the psychiatrist another person was to join the group. Preparations were duly made in that the admission of the new member was discussed with the group and his suitability for membership ascertained. The new member was informed of the group's progress and what the general norms of behaviour were. He was then introduced to the group and for several weeks the members were kindness itself to him ... then there was a distinct cooling in their attitudes though they were always polite. The leader could find no reason for this and could get no response to either direct questioning about it or by hinting that he would like to know what was wrong.
>
> Eventually, one of the members, in the course of a discussion with the leader on a different topic, muttered something like 'Well he hasn't talked you know ... he hasn't said a thing ...'
>
> It dawned on the social worker that the group, over the weeks, had established a norm of 'confession' as the price of acceptance. The 'new' member was discreetly informed of this and at the next session he began his contribution by saying 'I think I ought to tell you about myself'. He was listened to in interested silence and then the questions started.

114

From that moment he was a full member of the group with access to all their secrets and counsels. Needless to say the leader made a point of bringing out into the open the initiation rite and of suggesting that the group might in future help people to see what was required of them.

This kind of situation is very common. In fact some group leaders make a point of using ceremonies to emphasize that something is happening, to draw attention to it, and so make members aware.

It is important to recognize that anyone is at his most vulnerable when in transition from a state of security to a state of uncertainty. The whole problem of the 'new' member is of this order.

Another point which this example shows clearly is the difference between an open group and a closed one.

Open and closed groups

Open groups are those groups which never close their doors to the admission of new members. This means that they are constantly concerned with the 'new' member problem. Members leave and members are added so the problem of saying goodbye to someone who has worked with you for a period of time is also found in these kinds of groups.

Such groups never seem to develop the intense relationships which closed groups do, but they do have some difficulty maintaining a sufficient number of members as a 'core' to transmit the group culture, i.e. the norms and standards and values that the group has developed over the time of its existence. In this sense the nature of the group, e.g. either open or closed, can be seen as a constraint, but not one that is insurmountable. In fact the very nature of the difference can be used in order to achieve certain effects.

A group of people who have found difficulty in making and breaking relationships will get much more practice of how to do this effectively in a group which is open than in one which is closed and thus sheltered from newcomers and leavers. Likewise people who need the support of a few ongoing relationships so that they can develop the ability to trust others will be better served in a group which has a static membership.

Recognizing that the open or closed nature of a group creates peculiar possibilities means quite simply that such possibilities are taken into consideration right from the planning stage of the group and not discovered as problems halfway through the group's life.

Recording

Recording a group has always been a very sore point with group workers for a variety of reasons. First, it is absolutely essential and cannot be ignored. The ability that any one person may have to keep track of the interactions of several people, especially when he is involved in the same process as he is trying to recall, is at best severely limited. At worst it is disastrously biased and selective.

As we shall see later the efficiency of the group leader will depend to a large extent on his ability to make critical judgements based upon his understanding of the situation which faces him. The only way in which he can be in any way sure that he has the situation clear is for him to have been making continuous assessments of the progress the group has made, and this means seeing the large movements of the group which are the processes as well as the small and more immediate movements which go to make up the large ones.

This cannot be done over any extended period of time, if the activities of the group have not been recorded in some way which allows the group leader access to a continuous record to refresh his memory before every group session and to plan his work on the basis of knowledge rather than assumption.

The process of working with a group may be very involved and subject to vexations and sweat-producing problems. But this is no reason for the designed approach to be less than logical. And it is logical to realize that some form of recording is necessary.

The muddle and confusion can only be made worse if an unsystematic approach is used in this situation.

To be brutally frank right at the outset there is no substitute for the practice of 'recall in tranquillity', i.e. to sit down and record what has gone on immediately the group has finished using whatever notes have been made during the course of the group. All one can really do then is to develop a form of note taking during the group which is compatible with what one needs to do afterwards.

Changing role of the group leader

It is not always easy to assess what has happened to a group nor what the appropriate method of leading may be. In an article written in 1966, Kenneth Heap told the following story of a group worker's failure to recognize the signs of change.

The worker had set up a group, which was a social club, specifically to cater for the needs of elderly men who were becoming increasingly socially isolated. She proceeded to meet each of the men she deemed might benefit from such a club and established a good working relationship with each of them. She used this relationship, which she described as 'they made me feel like a loved but managing daughter', to generate good interaction among the group members and operated herself as group leader. As the men found common purpose and became identified with the club they began also to take over its running. After some months the worker had not noticed that their dependency upon her had changed. Heap ends the story thus:

> After some months the members asked her, with guilt and discomfort, if she had not more important things to do than spending an evening per week with them. They would 'well understand' if she 'decided to leave them to get along alone now'.[2]

This is a very clear indication of the need to keep abreast of

2 Kenneth Heap, 'Social groupworker as central person', *Case Conference*, vol.12, no.7, 1966, p.28.

the development of a group. It is also a good illustration of the responsibility that comes to the person who decides to create a group for the purpose of some kind of perceived need. It cannot be stressed too much that once the group so created begins to function, then the need which brought it into existence has to some degree been changed and the style of leadership needs to be cognisant of this fact.

An example

Stage three Operation The basic contract was now to use the group as a model for learning about group processes in general and to accept as a bonus any personal growth, i.e. any increase in personal awareness which resulted from this. This last point is very crucial. An element of deceit can too easily emerge here. Many groups which are started for purposes other than personal growth seem to turn into awareness-exploring groups. Now this is not fair for any number of reasons. First, several of the members may not have contracted for such a group had they known that this is what it was going to develop into. Once in, it is a very difficult thing to opt out because the group pressures can be very strong. Such members have thus had a very good lesson in being conned and whatever level of trust they may have started to develop will certainly be stunted by this kind of realization.

I have no intention of detailing the day by day operation of this group. An example of one of its sessions will be found at the end of chapter 1. Suffice it to say that the principle acts of leadership were divided into three stages:

1 Most effort in the early stages was put into the slow transfer from didactic teaching to experiential learning. Thus a large amount of information was still being conveyed but it was now made relevant to what was actually happening in the group at the time. When the group were trying to decide whether the behaviour of one member was appropriate and conformed to the aims of the group, the informational

input was related to the ways in which groups establish norms and standards of behaviour. When yet another member was being challenged for wanting to take over the group, the input related first, to concepts of social power and second, to acts of leadership, and so on.

2 In the middle period the effort was divided between maintaining the group as an entity over the various breaks which occurred (vacations etc.) and encouraging the members to make their own inputs based upon their own experience and learning. As a member would start to explain what he or she saw happening in the group, other members were encouraged to contribute so that the previous centrally focused group started to become much more open and to rely on all its resources rather than just one.

3 The third period was characterized by a withdrawal of leadership acts on my part which were of a controlling nature and the substitution of acts which were much more of a working nature. This meant that different members took charge of the group at different times; that my contribution in terms of the amount of time I actually spent talking decreased rapidly; that the analysis of what was happening depended upon some member of the group feeling moved to deliver himself of his observations; that the sense of accountability of each member from the group as a whole increased enormously.

During this period the group drew much closer together and started to spend some of their precious spare time in each other's company. They began to feel that they were a unit and opposition from other areas of the course tended to reinforce this feeling. I set tasks outside the group for them which could have been done in any of several ways ... they chose to do it as a group and to submit a group result ... each member standing or falling on the quality of their united work.

The insights into the way that they worked as a group came fairly thick and fast at this time. The problem was how to find the time for them to be able to relate what was happening to their knowledge of what happened in groups generally. Even so, the pressures outside the group continued to exert influence and the level of trust did not develop beyond a level which facilitated their learning. The personal growth bonus was thus quite small and not the same for each of the individuals. Relationships became more open and some friendships blossomed mildly. I was more and more treated as someone who could be trusted and the level of warmth in the group developed.

The problem of the assessment was solved by the comment being made upon the performance of the group as a whole rather than on its individual members. After all the purpose of the group was to learn about group processes and this could just as well be accurately measured in terms of the group as a whole as of individual members.

7 If you take it on, it's your responsibility

However a group leader tries to run his group whether by leaving the group to sort out its difficulties with minimum interference on his part or by being very directive, there is no escaping one basic fact which is that the person who called the group into existence has a continuing responsibility for it as long as it exists.

This brings into question all the various facts about leadership, which is indeed a very vexed subject and without doubt one about which most has been written in the literature on working with groups. This is not the place to go into the many theories which have been put forward about leadership, and which can be read about in textbooks. What I want to suggest is that it is preferable to leave the whole question of leadership in favour of a look at what might be called leadership acts, for the simple reason that in any group not only the designated or natural leader will make moves to shift the group in a given direction but so will many other members. The only qualifications needed for making this kind of move are that one can see that some kind of move is necessary, that one feels that one has some kind of answer to offer, and that it is worth taking the risk to offer it.

In essence then we are talking about pieces of behaviour displayed by members of the group which are designed, or at least have as their basic motivation, the perceived need to move the group in one direction or another. This means that we can look at the kinds of such acts more or less irrespective of who makes them.

Much has already been said about the need for leadership and the problems which underlie its acceptance as necessary in our society. Suffice it to say here that leadership acts which move the group towards the achievement of its avowed goals are to be encouraged and those which move it away from such achievement should be discouraged. The problem, as all group workers know, is to be able to decide which is which and to be able to recognize the good moves when they occur. They do not always advertize their presence upon first appearance as being what they eventually turn out to be.

In a sense then this is what I mean when suggesting that responsibility lies with the people who take on the business of trying to move the group, whoever they are.

One of the main problems with regard to leadership is concerned with what the helping professions sometimes call the 'conscious use of self'. This rather elaborate phrase tends to mean that in working with people it is necessary to be aware that the instrument with which one is working is oneself. There are habitual behaviours which have to be overcome and customary responses which have to be monitored in the pursuit of group effectiveness. For instance any leader will most probably be able to verbalize quite well. This is a very useful asset in our verbally oriented society. But when this fact intrudes too much in a group situation, it automatically precludes the participation of other members who are not able to fight their way into the conversation.

There is thus a barrier between one's own habitual behaviour and that which is appropriate to managing the group.

There is also a barrier between knowing and doing, which has to be overcome.

Leadership acts

I suppose that these can be divided into three main areas. There are those leadership acts which are working moves. Now these are basically concerned with keeping the group as a functioning unit and may be concerned either with the task which the group is trying to achieve or with the relationships of the members. Second, there are acts which are concerned more explicitly with control, with for instance encouraging behaviour which takes the group towards what it is trying to achieve and alternatively trying to stop or reduce those acts which are seen as preventing the group from doing this. Finally there are acts which are taken in the light of self-preservation which in some senses are not leadership acts at all except in so far as they can affect the other members and set a model for them to follow.

Working moves

The difference between task and relationship leadership acts is widely reported in the literature and is in fact often referred to as a clear distinction between kinds of leadership.

No group will work together if it has not come to terms with the problems inherent in a collection of people co-operating with each other to achieve some end result. If people are directing considerable energy to maintaining their own safety, then the same energy cannot also be directed to working at the task. As we have seen earlier, there is a great need for a group to develop an appropriate level of trust so that all its energies can be devoted to task performance.

A group of students whose main task was to use their own group in order to learn some of the ubiquitous facts about groups found that they were unable to proceed beyond the point of discussing the structure of their group. Time after time with the best intentions in the world they could only try to establish the rules under which they were prepared to proceed to the main task. Even this eluded them. They could not even agree about the way in which they would proceed. Eventually after many weeks of this kind of procedure one member ventured to say that he was unable to be open about what he wanted the group to achieve because he was awed by the experience and qualifications of other members of the group, which he perceived as far exceeding his own.

Once this point was out into the open it was evident that many other members of the group had similar feelings of inferiority which made them very cautious. Now the problem could be discussed and dealt with.

Intervention

However much we may try to avoid this issue we have ultimately to face the fact that groupwork is an interventive and manipulative process. The continuum of leadership goes from what is called directive-controlling activity at one end to non-directive at the other. This point has been discussed at length elsewhere. All I would say here is that anyone who thinks that in any real sense the non-directive end of the continuum implies no leadership at all is a con-man, and the person he is conning most is himself. One's very presence in a group affects the behaviour of others and theirs affects us. Whatever knowledge and understanding of group processes and of human behaviour a member possesses will guide his actions even if it causes him to withhold what in other circumstances he would have offered. His behaviour is selective and must therefore influence the behaviour of the others.

If leadership is recognized not so much as a specialized function, solely the perquisite of one person, but as residing in acts which any member of the group may make, then the designated leaders will be the people who make more leadership acts than others, based upon their greater expertise and knowledge. If and when other members develop group skills, then the number of leadership acts a designated leader may make will tend to decrease. It has always appeared to me to be totally unethical for such a leader to unload his obvious responsibilities on to people who must by the nature of things be more unaware of what is involved than he is, unless this act is part of a well-thought-out scheme to introduce people to the art of leadership. Let me give an example of what I mean.

A group leader says to his members at the beginning of some group exercises that they have a clear right not to take part in what is about to happen if they so wish. This can be seen as an indication of the leader's understanding of the natural anxiety of the members about something which may be unfamiliar but about which they have some fears. The responsibility to join in or not to join in has been put upon the individual members. But has it? On what basis can such a choice be made? Without experience and knowledge there is little logical basis. Can it be made on emotional grounds? Of course it can, but do we clearly understand what they are? Is it possible to know what pressures brought individuals to the group in the first instance or what pressure kept them there when they came? If one member feels he would like to opt out, how far is his behaviour going to be influenced by his perception of the kind of response such an act will elicit from the others and how much it matters to him?

We know that expectations that people have of a situation are created by a complex of factors and straight information of intent is interpreted in the light of this complex. It is my contention that it is the responsibility of every group leader either to contain the responsibility for the decisions within himself or to use such situations to enhance the understanding of the group members of the complex nature of the pressures involved, in other words to prepare them to accept personal responsibility in the light of understanding or at least of enhanced appreciation. Why? Because by becoming a group leader, by convening a group, by working with an existing group he has already consciously intervened in the lives of others and as such must bear the responsibility for the consequences of his actions. It is of no matter that his intentions were of a benign nature, the conscious act of intervention, a deliberate interference in the lives of others, whether at their request or based on some concept of conferring benefit, entails responsibility for the consequences. A chain of actions has been set in motion that would not have occurred in that form without the conscious intent of the instigator. In many areas of everyday life this is of little consequence because rightly or wrongly we assume sufficient knowledge on the part of those involved to make their involvement or otherwise a conscious choice. After all, the basic skill of the cheat is to ensure that his victims believe that they have sufficient information on which to base a logical and conscious choice when he knows in fact that they have not. But of the complex processes of human interaction, few people can be said to possess even a limited understanding. The case of the group worker is clearly that of being a one-eyed man in the kingdom of the blind.

There are thus two active and one passive possibilities. Let us consider the third first and get it out of the way. If possessing some knowledge of group dynamics, there is no intention to use it either for or against the interests of others, then the ethical considerations become almost academic. Of the two remaining possibilities one is to assume a paternalistic attitude of superior wisdom and to apply one's knowledge and skill, like the doctor, apparently for the benefit of others, without in any way attempting to enhance their understanding of what is involved. The other is to apply one's knowledge and skill to the generation of increased understanding on the part of others, so that they truly appreciate what is involved and can make choices based upon understanding thus assuming a real responsibility for themselves and not one based upon ignorance or half truth.

In the light of this we can now look at the process of intervention in the group situation, bearing in mind that either of the two active processes may be involved or even a continuum from one to the other as circumstances change.

It would tend to follow from what has been said so far that intervention comprises leadership acts and that these are not necessarily the prerogative of any designated leader. I think it would be helpful to isolate for scrutiny four different categories of leadership acts.

1 Those acts which seek to smooth relationships and establish and maintain the possibility of working together.
2 Those acts which are deliberately initiated to move the group towards the achievement of any tasks it may have,
3 Those acts which deliberately exercise control over the whole group process, are directive and tend to be long-sighted and goal-directed, and
4 Those acts which are concerned with personal survival and initiated by one person to enhance his security.

Before we look at these leadership acts in some detail, it must be remembered that usually intervention is designed to change something which is occurring. There are exceptions for example when what is occurring is fine and intervention is made to stop change taking place and to ensure a continuation of what is already happening. The number of ways of achieving change in addition to this is rather small. Behaviour can be enhanced, that is encouraged, diminished, i.e. reduced, changed to something else by the introduction of some new factors, or eliminated by the total change to new factors.

To complicate the matter somewhat it must be stated that the attempt to change may be directed in different ways. For instance one person may be making all the running and moving the group further and further away from its basic objectives. The introduction of change could come about by diminishing, eliminating or changing his contribution, or by encouraging the contribution of others, by bringing in other factors from outside the group, and so on. In short, intervention can be directed at individuals, sub-groups, the whole group or even at factors outside the group, e.g. the environment, key people etc.

Smoothing relationships

It must be apparent from what has been said so far that our society does not breed people who will work happily together. It does create people who are suspicious of strangers and even of loved ones, who are concerned so much to appear acceptable that they anxiously carry everywhere a fear of being exposed as different by unforeseen circumstances. Therefore it is not surprising that in any collection of people, particularly of strangers, an enormous amount of energy is devoted by everyone to ensuring that they are safe in whatever way the individual has discovered to work in similar situations in the past. Equally unsurprisingly, therefore, until some degree of security has been established, the amount of energy available for working together is diminished by the amount devoted to defence.

In a prison, a group of women was formed of prisoners who had long-term sentences. The objective was to facilitate the exchange of information about the ways in which the long spell of incarceration could be coped with. The group appeared keen and enthusiastic and enjoyed the weekly sessions, but never seemed able to tackle the task which had been contracted at the beginning of the group, despite urging by the group leader. Gradually it emerged that the leader had assumed that being part of the small prison system the women would all know one another well and that well-developed relationships would exist between people with a common bond. This proved to be almost the reverse of the fact as the women's relationships were limited to pairings and they were, if anything, more suspicious of each other than they were of the leader who was a probation officer. As they were able to establish working relationships so they were able to address themselves to the task and to reduce their presenting defences.

Because this was a situation in which many constraints operated against the development of appropriate trust between the members and between them and the group leader, the latter had to use the technique of selective reinforcement. Thus as behaviour appeared which seemed to indicate the beginning of trust in either of the two major areas, the leader encouraged it, making sure that the behaviour was made explicit and any warm feelings attached to it known to all. The leader also offered his own behaviour as a role model of the kind of norms which he believed would facilitate the development of working relationships. As a representative of authority he was the obvious target of suspicion, and was accused of being a spy, even a friendly one, or some kind of researcher. Where experience and knowledge cannot provide a credible answer to the kind of questions the women in this group were asking initially then fantasy will, and the nature of the fantasy is dependent upon the fantasizer's perceptions of the situation.

Elsewhere in this book emphasis has been laid upon the fact that a collection of people, the same time, and space does not necessarily constitute a group in the sense of being a unit with all that this implies. Much work needs to be done in turning that collection into a 'group', and basically that work is concerned with the establishment of working relationships which in turn will free energy to devote to the task in hand.

Getting on with the job

Of course there is no point at which it is possible to say 'before this the group did not work as a unit and after this it did'. At least that is so in my experience. What tends to happen is that at any time the collection of people is able to achieve something — the more threatening the task, the more co-operation required, and the more devotion to the group — the less likely the group are to achieve much progress in the early stages of their existence. This does not and should not ever prevent a leader from encouraging behaviour which he sees as task-oriented, unless he also sees that such behaviour is counter-productive in the sphere of relationships.

In a committee where the structure is very clearly defined it is always noticeable that members can work quite well together, provided that the matters under discussion have little or no direct relevance in a personal way to any member present. The structure creates the possibility of working together. When issues which do concern members personally arise, then the structure has to be reinforced and often even then cannot contain the emotions aroused. Because a committee is not usually a group in the strictest sense of the word, but a collection of individuals bound by a set of obvious rules, there is not often the degree of trust present which would contain such emotions and permit their expression and a working through of the problem.

Task-oriented leadership acts are concerned with getting on with the job in hand. Thus some members are more aware of those matters which impinge upon job completion than others, probably largely because of the personality factors which are involved or because of the degree of absorption with the group's progress or lack of involvement with other processes. Thus some members are very conscious of the fact that time is slipping away, of the need for further information, advice, help etc., of the need for checking on what has been so far achieved, of the need to encourage others to produce ideas and discuss them, to perform tasks relevant to the group's overall aim, and so on. When these perceptions are verbalized, they contribute towards getting the job done, they are guides, nudges, indicators of loss of direction or of impetus, and valuable in restoring the group's energy to the channel of goal achievement.

It must be obvious that either of the two categories of leadership act set out here can be performed by any member of the group who has the perception to see what is needed. In groups where members have little group experience it must fall to the leader to initiate acts of this nature and to encourage others to follow suit up to the point when members become aware of their responsibility.

A group of church members had gathered to make a decision about joint services with a neighbouring church. The minister very carefully opened the meeting by explaining what was involved. He also pointed out that a decision had to be made at this meeting in order that it could be passed to the neighbouring church committee in a few days' time. As the members felt strongly about the issue the discussion was at times heated and reiterative. The minister drew his members back to the task in hand by summing up what had been said for and against and by asking whether everyone was prepared to take a vote on the matter. Towards the end of the meeting he began intimating that time was running out. The committee members eventually faced the necessity of making the decision, realized they had exhausted most of the arguments and voted on the issue.

The exercise of control

Almost inevitably the acts which come within this category are those of a skilled and knowledgeable leader. Control implies a very wide concept of the group's existence, a view which is comprehensive enough to take in the immediate action and to see it in the context of what it will develop into. Thus control implies being able to assess which of the group's larger processes will be valuable to it, which may be detrimental, and which may be of little or no significance. The kind of long-sighted view necessary to make this kind of assessment comes only from experience of trying and failing and of trying and succeeding ... It is rarely the kind of ability found in people without experience and training, though in some areas of group life people seem to have an instinctive knowledge of which processes should be encouraged and which should not.

With every new group a skilled leader is faced with a whole series of complex possibilities. Until he has tested and tried some of them he cannot fill in areas of this complex as known. Gradually he recognizes response patterns and shapes, he becomes increasingly able to predict with some accuracy what the long term outcomes will be. At this stage he can, if necessary, moderate the behaviour of the group to facilitate the growth of those patterns which will best serve the ends of the group.

For example a group leader may well find that his totally inexperienced members expect that everything will stem from him. But the purpose of the group may well be that they should learn to be aware of group processes so that they can choose what they would like to do with them. In short to move the group towards becoming self-directing. In order to change the dependency set of these members, the leader must take a long term view of what processes will best meet this end. Paradoxically he may choose to exert such overall control that his control will be recognized by the group members, this recognition being part of their learning process which can then be adapted to decreasing the overall control exercised by the leader.

The processes which were identified in chapter 3 are usually the focus of any attempts at control. This is because the processes are fundamental to the group and they are big as opposed to the small patterns of immediate interaction and therefore to influence them implies having a larger and more permanent effect.

Basically the group leader has at his command a series of possible intervention techniques which he will use as judgement directs, bearing in mind the capabilities of the group, its level of development, and the aims it has set. It may seem trite to say this, but in all simplicity, the techniques are mainly concerned with keeping going things which are effective, stopping things which are destructive, reducing the effects of things which are not helpful or changing them to something more useful, and finally initiating and encouraging the development of positively beneficial acts. Of course this is much easier to write about than it is to do, and is complicated first, by the possibility of wrong assessment of the value of the behaviour and second, by the mode of intervention.

After several sessions the group had begun to gel. 'I feel that I can tell you about the fears I had on joining this group', said one member. The leader felt that this was a move in the right direction and encouraged the member to speak out. The encouragement was too positive, the member became embarrassed at becoming the centre of attention when in fact she had been speaking her thoughts aloud, and dried up.
The leader's assessment had been accurate as far as it went but had missed the nuances of the personal situation. However not all was lost, the leader recorded in his mind that a breakthrough in group trust could not be very far away and that he needed to remain very alert.

The stimulation or retardation of processes can be achieved in several ways sometimes by a combination of efforts. Again put very simply the desired movement may be achieved by attempting to modify the behaviour of an individual member whose current influence is great, or of a sub-group or of the total group. The final influence situation is the possible involvement of factors outside the group.

In the example given above the leader was attempting to encourage the behaviour of an individual which was clearly heading towards what he felt was desirable. It is always risky to do this with one member especially in the early days of a group, as that person may well be out of step with the majority and gain no support when exposed as a pace-maker.

Sometimes individuals seek support from fellow members and when they get it, a 'pairing' has occurred. If the pairing becomes an established fact, then a sub-group has formed and other members may join it or oppose it at different times. Some experts maintain that most of the worthwhile changes in a group come from powerful sub-groups. Whether this is true or not is not very important because the group leader can use his influence to affect the behaviour of the sub-group for the benefit of the group, as he can with the individual.

> *T.* I don't think you should have said that — it wasn't nice.
>
> *J.* We're not here to be nice — anyway other people have said what they thought.
>
> *B.* I didn't mind what John said — in fact I was thinking along those lines myself — I'd often thought that maybe — you know — I sounded a bit uninterested — not that I *am* uninterested really. I just — well you know what I mean?
>
> *T.* Are you sure that you didn't mind?
>
> *B.* Oh! no — not at all really — I...
>
> *S.* I didn't get the impression that Betty was upset by what John said.
>
> *B.* I wasn't — really.
>
> *C.* I think that as long as Betty didn't mind then (*Betty shakes her head and smiles*) maybe we can sort of accept that it's O.K. to say things like that.

T.	That's O.K. by me — I just wonder if it wouldn't — er — be, you know, better if the way things like that were said could be — er — a bit gentler — you know nicer?
S. and C.	*together nodding agreement,* Maybe — as long as we don't wrap it up too much.
Group leader	It seems as though Sally and Chris are suggesting that personal comments are O.K., providing they are made gently?
C.	That sounds soft — perhaps I don't mean gentle ...
S.	No, more a kind of statement of what one sees — is that it?
Group leader	There can be little quibble with saying what you see — it's a statement of fact about your perception and not about the person you are talking about ...

The group leader here was encouraging Sally and Chris in their exploration of what was an acceptable method of making personal comment. In terms of processes he was attempting to establish a norm of behaviour by enhancing and encouraging the contribution of the small sub-group of Sally and Chris, having assessed that Betty who had been the focus of the interchange was more than half way inclined to agree with the conclusions of the sub-group. Interestingly enough, information was being fed in at a point where it was relevant, i.e. that personal comments can be made in hurtful or constructive ways — the latter usually by referring to what one perceives rather than by making a bald statement that something *is*. Perceptions can be inaccurate; statements have an element of challenge. Thus, 'You are behaving in a very irresponsible way' is a challenge however true it may be and will no doubt provoke a defence which is not the best way to promote a possible change in the observed behaviour. Whereas to say that the behaviour appears to you to be irresponsible is a statement of what you have seen and what you feel and is not a direct challenge. This is not to say that when

134

relationships in a group are well developed that direct challenges are not possible — they are, but then the mechanisms for dealing with the possible conflict to the benefit of all concerned will probably exist.

The possible range of leadership acts which are of the nature of control can be displayed as follows:

These acts are achieved by:	*the behaviour of:*	*to modify one or more of the group processes:*
1 stopping	1 individuals	1 interaction
2 reducing	2 sub-groups	2 development
3 keeping going	3 the total group	3 structure
4 encouraging	4 external factors	4 sub-group formation
5 changing the focus of	5 a combination of two or more of the above	5 goal formation
		6 decision-making
		7 norms, standards, and values
		8 cohesion
		9 group influence
		10 climate

and require foresight and an accurate assessment of the value of the behaviour involved in achieving the long term operational aims of the group.

Often processes will be affected by drawing the attention of the total group to what is happening and bringing pressure to bear to change. For instance the leader can draw attention to the fact that the climate of the group is changing, becoming flat with enthusiasm dying away. This is obviously not the responsibility of any single member, and it must therefore come under consideration by the whole group and if possible a change be created more beneficial and supportive of the group's purpose.

No group is an isolate entity — it is affected by the environment in which it exists and in turn supplies stimulus to that environment. The members bring feelings, beliefs, and behaviour patterns into the group and take out attitudes and understandings developed within it. Therefore it stands to reason that another way of affecting processes within the group may well be brought about by intervention in selected external factors.

A group had been formed by a social worker for the purpose of introducing some local parents to the idea of becoming foster-parents. As the group had been founded on the basis of *interest*, one female member was discovered to have had a considerable amount of *experience* of fostering, whereas all the other members had none at all. This one woman dominated the proceedings and could not be dissuaded. The group was beginning to fall apart because of uncertainty and divided loyalty. The social worker discussed the problem with her superiors and the experienced foster parent was withdrawn from the group on the basis that she would be more valuable in another context.

This was an example of the use of outside factors in order that the group could begin to function. The unfortunate part was that the personality of the experienced parent made it too risky to attempt to involve her in a positive way by using her experience.

Of course leadership acts which exercise control over the group like these can come to be used by any member of the group once the necessary understanding and assessment skill is available. I would make two points about this which are:

1 That directive leadership should not be shirked on the grounds that it is reprehensible to attempt to control others.
2 That leadership acts require skill and understanding and it takes time to procure these, time which can often only be obtained during a period of security when someone else is monitoring and controlling the overall situation.

Now we must look briefly at the idea of self-preservation which is usually associated with the sense of loss of control.

Loss of control and self-preservation

Personal security makes life very complicated for the beginning group leader. Whatever his role, whatever his aim, one thing inevitably dawns upon him and that is that he is on his own until such time as the group accept him for whatever values they perceive he has. Numerically the leader is in a minority especially before the group has gelled into a working unit, when the expectations members may have of his performance is speculative and based to a large extent upon their own desires rather than on the reality.

How many times have group leaders found themselves in the situation of being expected to be experts with an omniscient bearing, upon whom the group members feel they are going to be able to rely utterly — when the leader's own feelings of his competence have not actually been very high? Alternatively there is the situation where the group members can be aggressive, challenging, having expectations which are much lower than the reality.

These situations and many like them are due expressly to the fact that anxiety is engendered by strange situations and then unfamiliarity takes over. Our responses vary enormously according to our past experience and what might be called our personal predisposition to an anxiety response of a particular character, e.g. overwhelming expectation of support from one whose status we enhance out of all proportion in order to convince ourselves of his potential for security, or aggressive intent which can serve to hide our own fears.

What has this to do with the dreaded loss of control which all beginning leaders fear? Well quite simply the more anxious a leader is about his own shortcomings, about his own performance, the more of his attention and energy he is going to devote either to securing his position, disguising his uneasiness or quite simply to thinking and feeling his way through his anxiety.

The crunch point comes here — and the decision is important. Are the group members going to be turned right off by a clear recognition of the anxieties of the leader? If the assessed answer is 'no', then there is no earthly reason beyond the fear of rejection why any leader may not make his apprehensions as much a point of discussion as the fears and expectations of everyone else.

Of course this can be a mistake both in timing and in confidence, and especially so, when a group believes and needs the leader to be an expert. The disclosure can only come as part of the growing awareness between all the members of a group, when they are 'strong' enough to realize that they are in fact working together and contributing to the group's life.

Loss of control then is a fear generated by an awareness on the part of the leader that he is at the beginning — that although he may have worked with groups a great deal, the carry-over of skill and understanding is not precise — the process of growing into a group needs to be gone through afresh each time. The essential point is to recognize the symptoms and recollect the cause.

It should now be clear why this chapter has the heading it has. Stated simply, if you conceptualize and create a group, then in a very real sense something which did not previously exist has come into being and you as initiator were responsible. If your aims are clear and you are going to direct what ensues from beginning to end, then there is no question that the overall responsibility stays with you. If however your aim is to enable your group members to accept responsibility for their own behaviour and the behaviour of the group, then the responsibility issue apparently becomes less clear.

In so far as you are successful in generating responsibility in others you then share overall responsibility with them, while maintaining all the responsibilities of being a person and member of the group. While operating as guide, enabler, facilitator, or whatever, you continue to exercise the responsibility consonant with that role.

Thus until you withdraw entirely from a group, responsibility is part of the chore. In fact the responsibility entailed in the nurturing role is much more subtle and delicate than that seen in the directive role. The facilitative leader is often a person much more conscious of the enormous responsibility he has taken on than the directive leader.

Most effective leaders find the area of practice which is most compatible with their personality, but are also aware that this comprises a range rather than a precise point on the scale. Most also know that in any one group they may need to cover the whole width of the range at different times in the group's life.

An example

Stage four Intervention As I have stated in general terms what kind of interventions were made in this group I would like now to use illustrative material from different parts of the same group to show different kinds of intervention.

Leader What did you do last week B.?

B. I can't really remember very much. I know I asked how these group sessions were going to teach us more about groups than teach us about ourselves.

Leader What do you remember J.?

J. Just that C. talked a bit more and that S. said that someone had got him down last term. I remember that. (*Laughter.*)

Leader Do you know why you remember that?

J. Yes ... No, I don't actually ... Oh! probably because you asked me what S. had just said when he said it.

H. I think we felt B. would learn more about herself by our responses to what she was saying. That was the crux of the argument.

Leader Yes. What was your contribution then H?

H. Well ... talking more about myself ... perhaps more than I've done throughout the sessions we've had since the beginning of term.

Leader And you got a response?

H. Yes.

As can be seen from this short example of actual dialogue the leader is the central figure through whom all the interactions occur. This is typified by the question and answer nature of the dialogue. Each person is drawn into the conversation by the offices of the leader except on very few occasions. If this kind of intervention continued, then no kind of sense of being part of the group would grow among the members who would feel that the power and domination rested with the leader alone. However this is in the early stages when there is a great need on the part of the leader to make the running and to get people used to the idea of just being in the group and of contributing to it, even if only doing this when asked a direct question. It gives them time to sum up what they feel about being there. Of course questions direct conversations as they require answers. While they have the merit of keeping things going they have the disadvantage of ensuring that the members do not contribute what is uppermost in their minds, but only what they deem to be the answer to the question.

In this next very short extract from the group records it can be seen that the interaction is now between the group members, and the leader's intervention is in no sense different in kind from anyone else's because he is just going along with what is happening. The events in the group are going towards the goal of learning about group processes and all he needs to do is interfere as little as possible.

> J. Could you imagine me ... if I was going it in the same situation and I couldn't do it either ... just asking somebody Is that clear? I suppose that's the obvious thing ...
>
> S. Yes, but I wouldn't like ...
>
> J. But I don't know why.
>
> H. Perhaps you were looking to P. to put your ideas over a little more simply for the benefit of those who weren't understanding? So that you directed your comments to her for support perhaps?
>
> S. No!
>
> *Leader* That's three people I have heard to say that they are not getting much support from the rest of

you in some way or other. I wonder why that is?

B.   I don't think I quite know why.

S.   I don't think I meant that.

Here the apparent coherence of the group has diminished, but they are thinking out the problem of mutual support for themselves. The leader's intervention is minimal and the question in his statement is open and not directive more a wondering than something requiring a direct response.

Apart from anything else this extract is a clear indication of the way in which people when they become absorbed in a topic pursue their own line of thinking in the presence of others, without paying too much attention to what those others are saying.

8 The last act

It must surely have been apparent from what has gone before that some groups come to an end. This is not true of all groups as they continue with altering membership for very long periods of time, e.g. clubs. One other thing must also be clear that where a group has been designed to achieve a special purpose that it should not just be allowed to fizzle when that purpose has to all intents been achieved.

Termination is then just as much a job which has to be gone through as the more often regarded one of setting a group up. In some ways it is more difficult because while there is the feeling of having to create something from nothing in the initial stages of starting a group, there may well be the sense of a 'natural' end when a group has completed its work. So that there is some excuse for the feeling that the group will run itself down as some extension of the natural process. While to a large extent this is true, there is also sufficient evidence to show that the opportunities for consolidation of the group's gains at this point

142

are very considerable and should not normally be overlooked.

One way of looking at this stage in a group's life is to recognize that from the very moment of conception the group will have been working towards this point. If the group has been set up to attain a given goal, then the point, distant in time, when it is achieved is also the point at which the group has no real reason for continuing its existence. However there are many occasions in which a group in the process of attaining one goal discovers that there is some merit in creating others which are then pursued. In other words new contracts are made as the group develops and begins to understand in a better or clearer way what it can achieve.

Of course not every group which is established with a goal to achieve is able to do so. Far from it. Many goals are set which are not within the capacity of the group, as constituted, to achieve; many reasons may exist why a group cannot attain all of what it sets out to do, e.g. sickness, lack of resources, too many negative factors etc. In which case it is the responsibility of the group leader to make some form of assessment and to offer to the group his opinions about the validity of the group's continued existence.

Termination has therefore to be considered in several ways. Open groups may never die. A club for instance stays in existence through membership changes. The problem of ending is therefore different and more a personal matter in an open group than it is in a closed group where ideally all start and finish at the same time.

The primary business of the last act is of course termination — the running down of the group because it has achieved its objectives. This is essentially based upon an assessment of the position and so we shall consider what is involved in this process first of all.

Assessment

Assessment is basically a practical judgement. In an earlier chapter I have pointed out that all leadership acts are based upon a judgement by the person making them that this is a valid thing to do. This implies that judgements are at the base of all human actions whether they are conscious judgements or not. Now this is far too wide a use of the word to be usable in the present context so that we must redefine assessment to a conscious process where a group member is actually aware of taking stock. This may take the form of saying out loud to the group what one thinks has actually occurred. As an assessment this has other recommendations. By spelling it out, what I think can be checked against what others think has happened and even if no increased objectivity results, at least all the members are aware of the difference of impact which the group events have had on different members.

In effect this kind of assessment is continuous and forms the basis for all actions members of the group take. It is also the basis of other forms of assessment in that the continuous stream of assessment eventually adds up to an evaluation of the total group. By recording the assessments which are made and comparing them with the actual outcomes the validity of the actions taken can also be judged and the value of the practice judgements checked.

To create a group takes a good deal of thought and preparation and to end one takes much more of the same kind of consideration than is usually realized. Why? Well in order for the gains which the group members have made to be retained, the period of termination has logically to include time to practise the transfer of knowledge, understanding, and skill into the field of everyday life. Much of what has been gained in treatment groups for instance can be lost because insufficient attention was given to consolidating gains before being exposed to the pressures of life without the support of the group.

Thus the time of ending the group is concerned with assessing how valid such a procedure would be. Of course if a contract has been formed which stipulated a given time for ending the group, then any assessment must be based upon a possible renegotiation. If one of the major constraints acting upon the group was the time limits available, then assessment about the desirable time for ending will take into account how much has been achieved in the allotted span.

Some groups do not achieve their objectives, some may not even succeed given more time or a different approach, and thus the end of the group may be brought about because assessment reveals these factors rather than those of achievement. On the other hand some groups achieve what they set out to do and then, having discovered what they are able to do, set out upon another stage in the life of their group.

At the end of the 10 sessions, the minders unanimously insisted they should continue for another period of 12 sessions. In fact it was felt that the group should go on for as long as the need was there ... So much has the self-esteem of the group grown that members have suggested that prospective child minders came along to their sessions and hear what a worthwhile job it is to look after other people's children, though clearly they will tell them the disadvantages as well![1]

This group had so enjoyed their initial sessions that they wanted not only to continue with more autonomy but to help other people do what they had done. They extended their activities to include talks by outsiders, evening meetings of parents and minders, and visits to other groups of minders.

A method which I frequently use in learning-groups, to bring about a constructive termination of the group, is to set up a series of evaluation situations which culminate in the whole group pooling its information and sharing its learning.

A group which had been established to learn about the processes of groups and the ways that these could be used in helping situations had reached its final day. The group had been resident together for four days and had done some fairly intensive studying and working together. Now the leader asked them to take time as individuals to make an assessment of what they had got out of the days spent together. These

1   Angela Simmons, 'Helping minders help themselves ...', *Community Care*, 1 January 1975, pp.21-4.

individual evaluations were then fed back to the members of the small work groups and finally the shared material of those groups was fed back to the whole course. The similarities and differences were most rewarding but above everything was the sense that the members had done everything in their power to integrate their learning before they left the group.

Clearly assessment at this time is not just a matter of finding out what one has learned, it is much more concerned with sharing. But it is also concerned with a well known but frequently ignored fact about learning which is the difference between what one feels one knows and what one actually knows in hard, cold facts. In group learning this distinction is not quite so important because one of the most important aspects of the learning process in this case is the actual sense of having been in a group experience. The actual feelings are a very important part of the total learning that takes place. Nevertheless it helps very much to try to state what other kinds of learning have taken place and it also helps others by emphasizing things they have learnt and also by reminding them of things they had forgotten.

So much for the group which has a very definite time limit in which to achieve a given task and which by definition would have to be a closed group. But what about the group which is going to go on for a long period of time and where the basic task is to exist for the benefit of its members? Such a group is by definition an open one and termination applies to the membership of individuals rather than to the life of the group itself.

The members of a psychiatric halfway hostel all formed part of a committee which administered the simple day by day routines of the hostel. This meant that each member was part of a very influential group which to a large extent controlled what could be done. Although each member also received attention from the psychiatrist and social workers, his discharge from the hostel and his entry into it were matters for discussion amongst the total group. Jobs which were allocated by the committee sometimes meant that members ready for discharge would be asked to wait until a substitute could be found to do their task. The group as a whole often were faced with the task of coming to terms with the loss of old established and very useful members of the community. Equally they had to face the fact that new members would arrive. A reception group was formed for this purpose.

In this situation the group was seen as an adaptation process for people who had stays as inpatients and needed time and help to find accommodation and work but did not require skilled nursing care. As each person came into the group, which was quite small, his needs as an individual were considered by the group but the main factor was initiation to the life of the group. The hostel could only run and provide a service if it were to be a largely self-running enterprise. Thus each new resident quickly came to recognize that his needs might only be served if the group was kept in existence by his efforts in combination with the efforts of others.

Termination in this kind of group meant that the period of adjustment to life outside an institution had been reasonably successful, that work and some form of accommodation were available and that the support system of a self-help group had been substituted for the encapsulating care of a psychiatric unit.

Perhaps the most significant feature of all forms of termination in a group is that which is concerned with preparation. After all when a person is joining a group he has to go through the experience of being accepted and of learning what the acceptable behaviour patterns of the group are. He is concerned with whether the group will accept him and he is concerned with whether he wants to accept the group. Later he becomes concerned with the amount of influence the group may have over him and he starts to think about how much influence he might want to exert. Perhaps even later still he recognizes that trust is an important part of group life and he becomes aware of the degree of liking he has for other members and how much they have for him.

The whole of this process of working into the group has to go into reverse when a member is leaving or when the group as a whole is closing down. The ties of liking need at least to be slackened and those with people outside the group strengthened. After all these are going to be the ones which will be most important in the near future. Then the influence of the group has to be lessened and here the learning which has taken place needs to have been integrated so that it can be used without the support of the group. Finally the actual presence of the member within the group has to be terminated.

Group members carry with them the memory of their time within a group, especially if it was a good time and helpful. This then acts as a reference group and serves as a store house of impressions ideas and feelings and also as a source of behaviour.

It can be seen from this that I am advocating that as much care should be taken with the ending of a member's attachment to a group as was taken with his arrival in it. Whatever the kind of group, if it had value for the member, then it is worth taking time and effort to ensure as far as possible that that value stays with the member after he has left. Too often once the supportive nature of the group has been given up and the care of the group leader left behind, the changes and the learning are seen not to have been integrated into the personality and experience of the erstwhile group member and the pressures of life can soon destroy their effect.

A philosophy of groups

I suppose that in some senses this section should be unnecessary. The way in which I perceive groups should have emerged clearly from what has been written here up to this point. However, at the risk of being repetitive I think it is worth the attempt to state clearly the basis of my thinking about groups and thus add to and reinforce what has gone before.

First, I do not believe that the use of groups is a universal cure-all any more than any other technique used by human beings. However I do believe that the concentration on an individual psychology until very recently has produced a counter-thrust in terms of social and group psychology. Both are extreme positions and need to be regarded with care. They are like the controversy which has raged for such a long time about the relative value of nature or nurture, a dichotomy which manifestly exists, but whose constituent parts are in no way mutually exclusive. Essentially *both* individual and group processes contribute to the development of each human being and the problem is only bedevilled by the claims of those who maintain that one is overall more important than the other.

If we accept that these two possible explanations of the forces acting on human beings co-exist, then the problem becomes how much of which exists in any given situation. In the area of the application of remedies to human ills, which approach, group or individual, is more appropriate? I think this is fairly easily determined and can be summed up by saying that a group is most useful as an instrument in those areas of human experience which are concerned with the need for acceptance and support, with co-operative endeavour either for work or pleasure, for the conveying of formulated information for learning, particularly about oneself and one's attitudes to others, and of course for learning about the ways in which groups function. I would subsume all these points under the general heading of 'support'.

The individual tends to operate much more effectively, not exactly in isolation, but more independently in all areas of human behaviour which can be called 'creative'. No one, to the best of my knowledge, ever created anything of value as a member of a group except those factors which pertain to the group, as for instance support or the reflection and exchange of ideas. Thus no painters ever created a worthwhile painting as a group. Of course there are many examples of groups executing paintings, the students of some master — like Rubens for instance, but the guiding genius and overseeing creative intelligence was that of the master and not the pupils. Likewise no book or piece of music, no drama, no truly creative work can be performed by a group except in similar circumstances, i.e. under the overall direction of a creative individual. Which brings me directly to a consideration of teams and computers.

149

Teams are groups in many senses. They recognize membership and the necessity of co-operation and of shared experience. But they demonstrate a kind of halfway stage between the self-directing group and the individual in that they are manifestly composed of individuals who are working to a plan usually conceived by an individual. A team illustrates the combination of support and creativity which is a necessity of such co-operative behaviour, which incidentally tends to be marred if not destroyed by *prima donna*-like behaviour of a member of the team.

Groups therefore do not think or create new ideas in the way that individuals do. The individual members of a group do the thinking and the creating and the group endorses, accepts, modifies, or rejects that thinking. A group thinks in the sense that individuals 'think' together and modify their behaviour in the light of what they see others produce. Such modifications may never have taken place, if each member had done his thinking in isolation, largely because he might never have known of them. Groups do therefore make decisions, but they do not create new ideas except as a stamp of approval on the offerings of individual members.

Computers offer a simple illustration of this fact. Any computer contains information placed there by a number of individuals. The computer can recall any required pieces of that information, scan the contents, compare any piece with other pieces with remarkable speed, but it cannot create what previously did not exist. It does not 'think'; it merely obeys the instructions given to it by a thinking human being. Of course the machine can frequently see correlations between pieces of information stored within it that human thinkers have not seen and create new knowledge in this way, but this is a function of the speed of correlation-making rather than any truly creative process.

In a way the whole business of group and individual is a problem throughout society. The individual who does not conform is frequently the producer of valuable ideas, whereas mass conformity to group pressures produces massive co-operative effort along accepted lines but few innovations. The society

150

which is able to use both forms to its advantage obviously stands to gain most by allowing freedom for non-conformers to produce ideas which enhance the quality of life for the conformers. Also obvious is the risk of creating an elitist society rather than a meritocracy or alternatively the banal mediocrity which stultifies conformist societies.

What arises from this is the fact that groups are microcosms of the society from which their members are drawn. If society can benefit from exploiting both individual and collective behaviour in an intelligent way, then conceptualized groups can benefit from exploiting collective action in those areas of human behaviour where it is known to be most effective.

Having used the word 'exploit', I feel bound to say something about leadership. More has been written about leadership than any other aspect of group behaviour and the concept of 'leader' bears various connotations in our society ranging from downright distrust to complete acceptance. Some people automatically respond to leadership by opposition to it almost as an unthinking reflex, supposedly on the basis that power is dangerous particularly if concentrated in one person's hands.

To go back a moment to the discussion on the individual and the group earlier in this section is to see that not only is it necessary to give the individual the scope necessary to exercise his abilities, but he should be positively encouraged so that others may benefit from his knowledge, insight, ideas etc. This is in no way to accept overall superiority in such people, but it is to accept superiority in those areas of their existence where superior knowledge, skill etc. exists even for a small period of time. If they do likewise, i.e. accept superiority in others when they are aware of lack of such skill or knowledge in themselves, then the ultimate use of existing potential becomes possible.

Thus leaders and leadership are not only necessary but should be highly skilled and effective. If the end product of such leadership is to develop self-help ability in others, then so much more essential is it that the people who take on leadership roles should be the most capable rather than that such roles should go by default to those less able because of suspicious attitudes towards power. There should therefore be no guilt attached to the effective performance of a leadership role whether this is seen as temporary or permanent, but only a desire to perform it as well as possible.

One final word about leadership. If I have given the impression that good leadership is only found in selfless acts for the benefit of others, then I must state categorically that I do not believe this to be so. Good leadership tends to exist in those skilled and knowing behaviours of leaders, designed to assist the group achieve its objectives and from which the leader should derive immense satisfaction and pleasure. This is the truly creative nature of leadership and it is far from pious to recognize that skilful work brings rewarding satisfactions. In fact this is very much in line with the basic thesis of satisfactions stated earlier. Not even the most dedicated leader in the world will continue to function effectively if he derives little satisfaction from performing the role. Let me make one other related point. In concentrating on the idea of leadership I have perhaps oversimplified and given the impression that there is only one kind of leader. This is obviously not so. Any person who has skill and knowledge to contribute, however small or apparently insignificant, can and should occupy the position of leader. This is the main reason that earlier I have concentrated not so much on leaders as persons, but on leadership acts which can be made by anyone.

What I have said here indicates briefly some of my own personal philosophy of groups. I believe that created groups are only effective in certain areas of human behaviour and that these areas should be clearly understood and defined. I also believe that groups are concerned with acts of leadership and that leadership can be learned and should be exercised with great skill and understanding and should provide rewarding satisfactions for the leader. If such acts of leadership are designed to be permanent, i.e. totally directive, or to lead to the group becoming responsible for its own direction, this is irrelevant, in so far as either, or any intermediate stage is appropriate for the task in hand. What is relevant is that such leadership

152

should be knowledgeable, understanding, caring, and effective.

An example

Stage five Termination and evaluation   The ending of a student group has been fixed well in advance because of the end of the course. So whether the group has achieved its task or not or at least whether it has achieved more or less of its task, it has to come to an end. Of course this has advantages and disadvantages. If an end point is known so far in advance, it becomes part of the life of the group that they know when the group is going to end. This means that the pressure of time can actually work to the benefit of the group by compelling them to move faster than if they had unlimited time.

Theoretically the end of a group should see leadership acts directed towards the members being able to back away from the group and involvement with it. This is the reverse of the starting moves which are designed to bring the members closer together. In the student group the increase in number of references to outside factors like work situations etc. was quite noticeable during the summer term. There was also a great deal of effort put into how they were going to be able to use what they had learned about groups and about themselves. This involved trying on the role of leader of the group and trying to produce given effects which were later analysed by the group as a whole.

The main consideration however was what the job situations they were going back to would allow them to do. Although this is eminently a practical consideration and very logical, it also forms the basis of emotional withdrawal from the group in preparation for working without it.

Alongside this consideration was another of almost equal importance which is the attempt to assess exactly what one has got from the experience. Allied to this is inevitably some element of criticism of the leader, especially if what one discovers one has got is not exactly what one had hoped to get either in kind or in quality. I believe that whether such criticism is entirely justified or not, and one suspects that it may be on most occasions, it forms part of the parting ceremony sparked off by some sense of loss or probably of time not used to full advantage for a large number of reasons. This is the time when the favourite phrase becomes 'If only...' which indicates a degree of regret.

The leadership acts of this stage then are directed towards helping group members say good-bye to the group and in reasserting themselves as independent operators. Of course one of the main factors in achieving this is still the old gambit of looking at what the group is doing. If the group members can see themselves actually withdrawing; if they can sense that the commitment of each person is decreasing; if they can see the attempts at consolidation of learning which are being made, then the learning process will continue.

It was interesting that during this period a fair amount of reference to the beginning of the group took place. For the first time members felt that they could clearly say what they had felt about joining the group in the first instance and how anxious they had been. It emerged that most had been waiting for others to make the first move towards a better state of integration, a situation which often occurs and can lead to stagnation if it is not broken. The feeling that their behaviour had been superficial and very defended was put forward, and criticism of the leader for not recognizing their dilemma sooner and doing something about it was also advanced.

Because the group had spent some time working through the nature of its own ending, when the last group session occurred it ended in much the same way as all the others. Friendly good-byes were said and some arrangements tentatively made for contact if and when it was needed after the course had finished. And then we all went our separate ways feeling quite kindly disposed to each other and it was all over.

Evaluating this group meant comparing it with others of a similar nature, taking into account what the members had said about it, and looking carefully at my own feelings. It had been a group which was slow to develop trust, but this is not unusual in such a group; several members had wanted to move at a much faster pace than others, again this is quite usual in such a group and tends to develop the braking power of the group rather than its accelerators. Finally there was my own learning as leader and the mistakes I had made clearly outlined by the students in their comments, mainly to do with assumptions I had made and with lack of perception about this particular group. At this point the cycle is complete.

9 Here, there, and almost everywhere

Although a large number of the illustrations used here are taken from social work practice, this is by no means meant to imply that groups are solely the instruments of professional users. In fact as the title of this chapter was meant to assert, the use of groups is very widespread throughout our society, and it is to the people who set them up that I am trying to convey some of the information which I hope might help them in their tasks. Take *Scope* for instance:

> The idea came to Lin when she was working on an educational research project in Yorkshire. She realized that if a mother was depressed her child's education would be affected ... She literally took to the streets, knocking on doors and talking to women with prams in shopping centres. Gradually she collected a group of mothers who agreed to get together and discuss their worries and experiences over a cup of coffee. And *Scope* began.[1]

1 Diana Guyon, 'At home on the estate', *Ideal Home*.

One person saw that there was a problem of loneliness and of possible depression for the mothers of young children and decided to do something about it. *Scope* is only one of hundreds of self-help groups which have been set up by people who realize that if they do not do something for themselves then nobody else will.

Basically all these groups have one very simple connecting link and that is shared experience. This stems from a recognition that several people can often achieve what one person finds impossible.

A simple rule of thumb which can indicate the possible need for a group or some other form of help is concerned with change. Thus where people are facing a situation which will bring about a large change in their accustomed style of life, then fear of the unknown, anxiety about the possible consequences, worry about whether coping mechanisms are adequate, frequently occur. At this point in his life one person may well be very pleased to meet someone who has passed this stage as well as a number of others who are just going through it. In the first instance he is presented with a person who has undergone the experience and apparently survived ... he can talk from experience about how it was achieved. In the second instance he is faced with people who are about to go through the same experience as himself but they bring to it different viewpoints about what is involved and also different ideas for coping. Within limits more people means more ideas and thus the possibility that ways of approaching a problem which individual members had not thought of for themselves are presented for their use. It is these factors of experience and the production of ideas which are successfully exploited in a large number of self-help groups. In many instances the only way which seems to work with people with maladaptive behaviour patterns, like drug addicts, is that they shall have a chance to live in society where they make the rules and they enforce them — a democracy where each member comes to realize that he is responsible for his own behaviour and for that of the community as a whole. Although specialists are used in some of these establishments, their role is frequently peripheral. It is apparently much easier for such a person to accept the necessary tough handling from someone he knows has been through the same situation himself than from someone whose knowledge, though probably wider, is not of a personal experience kind.

In 1968 Barry Sugarman wrote an article about the Phoenix unit at Littlemore Hospital, Oxford. In it he described a therapy module...

> ... in a formal group during which the attention of the group is focused overtly upon the problems of one individual. He or she is therefore 'the patient' for the time being. But there is unlikely to be any one other person who (even for this module) plays the exclusive role of therapist. Rather there are about ten distinguishable roles in this process of group therapy which are shared around. One group member may play several of them in the same session: several members may take turns in playing the same role: both may happen — all while the same person occupies the role of patient.[2]

With problems of the treatment of the mentally ill, with difficulties like addiction to drugs or alcohol; with problems of loneliness, of depression, of too much weight, and with a myriad others, groups are being set up to cope.

Sue Jennings in a delightful little book on remedial drama shows how she uses drama techniques with groups as widely disparate as immigrants, backward children, the disturbed, maladjusted and psychotic, the physically handicapped, severely subnormal and so on. She tells of a new group in a short-stay psychiatric ward who were very suspicious of her.

> The group began telling me how very bored they were — 'there's only the radio'. We began discussing radio plays and how they were made; it was then only a short step for the group to decide that we could make up our own play. They decided it was to be a Russian spy thriller — James Bond theme music provided the right atmosphere. We recorded

2 Barry Sugarman, 'The Phoenix unit: alliance against illness', *New Society*, 6 June 1968, pp.830-2.

the play on to a cassette tape-recorder and played it back at the end of the session. Apart from the change in attitude towards drama, in itself important, members of the group began to get up off their chairs spontaneously when various sound effects were needed in the play such as doors slamming or footsteps running down the corridor.[3]

Not only does this show that talk is not always the most useful activity for a group, but that adults whose attitude towards drama is that it is a child's pastime may well learn to benefit from it under skilled guidance. There is hardly a situation in which human beings find themselves which cannot be looked at in group terms.

It may be instructive to look at what all these groups have in common. Basically there is recognition that a situation exists which cannot truly be coped with by an individual. Of course this is sometimes just a matter of sheer numbers. Take a drama society for instance. The number of roles which are required indicates that a large number of people will be required to fill them. Essential decisions may well be made by a small number of these members in the form of a committee. Even here the committee is itself a special kind of group in which the rules of procedure are clearly outlined and not left to be discovered by the members as they work. A further simple point is that a group may be formed because the job which it is going to do just cannot be done, either in terms of the resources needed or of the time available, by one or two persons.

Recognition of common need seems to be another factor which gets groups off the ground. Social factors of course loom large in all groups and frequently form a great back-up to whatever original incentive existed. Some people join groups because they feel they will be mixing with people they would like to meet and work with, but others find that they join for some other reason and the social factor is an additional bonus. Shared experience has been stressed as an essential feature, but shared responsibility is often just as important. Where difficult

3 Sue Jennings, *Remedial Drama* (London, Pitman Publishing, 1973), p.66.

decisions have to be taken not only do more people offer the possibility of more possible solutions but also they offer shared responsibility for any decisions which may be taken.

Educationists have always used a group approach, though often not using the effects that groups can have to the full in removing blocks to learning or even in combining experience as mentioned above. Too often the use of the group has been based on the economy of numbers, that is information can be conveyed to a number of people much more economically if they are all in one place at the same time. The fact that such a group would have one central focus, that of the teacher, meant that little interaction took place between the members of the group at least in the formal teaching situation. Thus most of the group's dynamics were not used.

Groups are part of the environment in which they exist and nowhere is this more easly seen than in those groups which are created in residential situations so that one is in fact looking at a group living condition. We shall also look briefly at groups in use with the elderly and at groups used in medical and health care.

Groups in residential establishments

Many of the illustrations of groups given so far have been set in some institution or other. The reasons for this are not far to seek. Residential settings already define group boundaries clearly and visibly. There are people who live in the institution and there are those who do not. The whole nature of belonging is writ large and made very obvious even to the undiscerning. For this reason residential institutions offer the possibility of studying and of using what could be called 'group living'.

A second reason for the proliferation of groups in this kind of setting is the fact of having, in many cases, a captive audience. The potential group members are held within the boundaries of the institution and are thus, physically at least, available. Third, there is no way of truly escaping from the presence, or the effect of the presence, of others even in solitary confinement, so the interaction and the contact level are already high and may be intense, but may also be constrained by procedural rules which need to be learnt and which protect people from over-exposure.

The effort of gathering a group together, of selling the aims and purposes to prospective members, the bother of travelling to arrive at the place where the group is held and many other practical issues do not arise within a residential situation. Other factors like boredom, the availability of accommodation, of staff, of equipment do arise and tend to facilitate the formation of groups. The behaviour which can be discussed in a group situation may well be the immediate behaviour found in the inytitution. It is therefore topical and relevant and possesses the merit of being of interest to the participants.

The effect of the environment is of course also immediate and shows much more clearly than in group situations not in a residential setting. The ethos of the institution, the visible surroundings, the presence of others, the memories, experiences etc., all contribute to a conditioning process which can be very strong. This is in no way peculiar. We all modify our behaviour in the light of our perception of our surroundings, e.g., in church, in the pub, in law courts, at home etc. The perception of what is appropriate and of the possible sanctions for inappropriate behaviour are very strongly effective in controlling that behaviour.

One great problem of groups in residential situations concerns the factor of exclusion. In a very broad sense all groups are exclusive. By being a member of a group one is excluded from physical presence in another group at the same time. Also membership of a group defines those who are 'out' equally as well as those who are 'in'. In ordinary circumstances this matters only a little, for the people who are out, unless they have an overwhelming desire to join, do not see this exclusion as some form of loss. But in a residential establishment the demarcation, like many other factors, becomes that much clearer because of the confined and discernible space in which it operates. It is very easy to see which people belong to a group and which do not when the population is so small, defined, and to some extent much more visible.

Thus in a hospital ward those patients who attend certain types of therapy are known and easily recognized by those who do not. This poses two major problems for the group practitioner. First, if the group he creates constitutes less than the total population of a given institution, or even of a well defined part of it, then those not chosen will tend to feel excluded (they are excluded), and whether they are pleased about this or not, a distinction has been created.

Second, those selected, stand to be regarded as some kind of elite. If the selection process is rigorous, if the group is successful, even if it is enjoyable or different, depending on the general sense of well-being in the institution, those who attend will be regarded as different. They may be regarded as fortunate, they may see themselves as superior or more worthy or as having undergone something different. In this their perception is accurate, but it can be either constructive in creating a progression which is aspired to, or destructive in that it generates a sense of preferential treatment.

I am not saying that elaborate ruses should be practised to avoid this; on the contrary it is almost unavoidable. I am merely pointing out that any group practitioner should recognize that these influences are at work and need to be allowed for in any group strategy which he plans. To do otherwise is to find oneself faced with a group which generates powerful effects over which one has little or no control because they have not been foreseen, but which are very real constraints in residential situations.

Residential establishments present particular challenges to the group worker. In any circumstances a group has to be seen as an integral part of the milieu in which it exists. This has been stressed several times because in ignoring it group workers set themselves unnecessary problems which create the seeds of possible disintegration of any group so convened. In the residential setting these environmental factors are not only closer and ever present than in life outside, but they can more quickly operate to constrain anything within the organization which might appear to be unconforming.

In the residential setting as nowhere else it becomes apparent that groups created as an outlet, as a remedy, and which are external to the organizational structure like sticking plaster on a finger, have very little chance of being even minimally effective. In a hierarchical structure responsibility for decision-making is allocated at what are deemed to be appropriate levels. A group established in this structure cannot conceivably function as a decision-making unit at a higher level of responsibility than those who convened it, unless its purpose is to attempt to modify the structure by breaking it.

Where group members are offered the possibility of making decisions affecting their lives, then the feasibility of effecting any decisions so made within the structure should be real and not fictional. Otherwise the group will have achieved a phenomenally effective exercise in enhancing its own apparent powerlessness, and conversely demonstrated the placatory and off-putting nature of the group exercise. Clearly the non-verbal communication which arises from the actions and behaviour of those involved is demonstrably more effective than their words.

Groups of people living together may not constitute a 'group' in the sense in which this term has been used throughout this book. They may be a collection of people which can be seen as a 'group' because a very tangible boundary exists which defines their exclusiveness and separation from others. But this is not necessarily a 'group' boundary, acclaimed and accepted by the members as defining their sense of belonging; it may well be seen as an intolerable frustration.

Obviously smaller groups than the total institution can be shown to exist. It is well to remember however that some residential units are small enough to constitute an effective working group.

In a discussion with residential workers in which I was involved in 1973 some of the ways in which groups could be used in a residential setting emerged. They were listed as follows:

Type of group	Aim	Description
1 House meeting	(a) to funnel information	client organized
	(b) to create an information shop	shifting population
	(c) to support	common interest
2 Crisis meeting	to resolve a crisis	either total population or total client population
3 Total group experience		group living
4 Therapeutic group	(a) to foster self-understanding	may be either
	(b) to promote decision-making skills	selected (by staff) compulsory ad hoc
	(c) to promote coping skills	client centred or run by
	(d) to promote sensitivity to others	outsiders
5 Client organized groups	to socialize	
6 Organizational decision-making groups	to facilitate the working of the residence	residents' committee action groups
7 Opinion testing groups	to facilitate decision-making	
8 Discussion with external groups	to promote inter-group relationships	
9 Staff groups including external resource people	enhance contacts and efficiency	
10 Client-conflict resolution group	crisis resolution	smaller than (2) (staff established)
11 Contract group	to establish an agreed basis of working together	includes assessment meetings, selection, initiation (combination of staff / clients or either alone)
12 Management group	part of the organizational function	not everybody has a say here

Type of group	Aim	Description
13 Inter-hostel group	contact idea- and information-exchange.	usually geographically decided — similar to (8)
14 Activity groups	positive use of leisure time	camping, games etc.

This group also studied several continua which seemed relevant and upon which they could plot the position of their establishment (a) as it is, and (b) as they would like it to be. The purpose here was to indicate the restrictions the reality of a given situation (the constraints) would tend to impose upon the use of groups or other counselling techniques.

1 *The organization of the establishment*

Total group organization	Hierarchical or other organization which uses groups within the structure as a method of ensuring certain ends

2 *The orientation*

Treatment	Containment

3 *The style of the organization*

Autonomy	Directed

4 *The tolerance level*

Tolerant of ambiguity	Intolerant of ambiguity

The remaining continua (5 and 6) were seen as different from the first four in that they applied in a different way. In 1-4 the lefthand column entries are all related in some way as are those on the right. Thus any institution having a position to the right of any one scale will tend to have righthand positions on the other three.

But:

5 Active	Passive
6 Planned	Unplanned

seemed to the group to relate equally well to either side.

This exercise served well to illustrate the numerous possibilities of utilizing group procedures and processes within residential establishments and was a sound counterblast to the concepts either that groups have to be formally created or that they are something separate from the community.

Groupwork with the elderly

In the flood of literature about working with groups only a trickle is devoted to working with the elderly. Why is this? The first and most obvious reason may well be the obvious neglect which has surrounded services for the elderly for a long period of time. The medical aspects of ageing are catered for in the journals of the medical profession but there is little evidence of how the practical problems of coping with the elderly might be met.

Much of the blame may also be attributed to the generally accepted idea that the elderly, retreating into a second childhood, reduce their boundaries in an ever-intensifying withdrawal in reversion to an egocentric state. Such a withdrawal in younger people is not regarded as a good reason for not using groupwork, but is frequently offered as the main reason for admission to a group. This shows that where old people are concerned other factors are involved. One of these factors may be the attitude of our society to the old, based upon some vaguely held belief of the uselessness of the old and on a rapid decay of any powers they may once have had.

No doubt such a decline does take place; this is not questioned. What is questioned is how much more rapid the descent into senility is than it has any need to be. Is it not possible that if elderly people are given opportunities within their limits, they can perform at a reasonable level for much longer than is usually expected and that interest and abilities may even be enhanced in the short term?

Looking at what people have done in this field I find that four principal group activities have been used:

166

1 Group discussion
2 Group counselling
3 Activity groups and
4 Group psychotherapy.

Let us now look at what has been done in these areas and what the outcomes have been.

1 *and* 2 *Group discussion and group counselling* Discussion methods were used in order to promote informal groups, to identify the social structure in which the elderly people lived, and to enable them to become aware of the sub-systems and living units that existed.

The kind of problems discussed centred in the fields of personal relationships; current events; health problems; social problems; loneliness; death; ageing; religion; and the relationship of the group members to the leader.

The results of the application of these methods seems to have created an atmosphere of warmth, permissiveness, and acceptance. The elderly people were facilitated in their decision-making and there was evidence of enhanced initiative. Increased interest and dignity seems to have developed and a great improvement in appearance. The major gain was in support for each other as fellow human beings with increased abilities to communicate and to socialize.

Overall there was a decrease in the depression which tends to accompany the ageing process and with this a reduction in anxiety and feelings of inadequacy. Better use was made of the facilities offered to the elderly and in the treatment oriented programmes obstacles to treatment tended to decrease. Certainly where groups looked at the structure of their environment, more members were prepared to take part in decision-making and there was very frequently a redistribution of power away from the staff side.

Certain problems are apparent in this form of groupwork with the elderly, mainly along the lines of increased stress on members which tends to result in a number of drop-outs who

167

form a secondary group with a deadening influence within the establishment. It has also been noted that this kind of discussion group can be instrumental in increasing the dependency of some members, and is therefore counter-indicated in such cases. Termination of such a group is also difficult because it tends to form a focus in lives otherwise somewhat monotonous and routinely dull.

Finally there is some hint that such a group may have little or no value with the less intelligent and sensitive clients, who are not in the habit of talking about themselves or their problems.

3 *Group activities* The aim of groups with an activity as their basic method is quite simply to counteract the de-humanizing influence of institutional life, and as far as possible to involve the residents in the constructive use of some of their time. Interest groups focused round some particular hobby, discussion groups and recreational activities including team ball games were used. Mixed age groups were used in most cases in order that the advantages of mobility, vision, etc. were evened out.

The main criticisms which can be made against such activities may be listed as follows:

1 They occupy leisure time but tend to have little or no meaning in terms of the basic needs of the elderly.
2 They tend to trivialize and thus act counter to the avowed aim of maintaining the dignity of the aged.
3 They tend to appear condescending and childish to the clients.
4 They enhance the dependency of the aged upon the institution and on the worker.
5 They tend to foster the image of old people as socially useless.

Obviously groups of this nature have some value if it is only that someone is taking an interest in the aged. But the dangers listed above could and should be avoided by the use of judicious enquiry into the resources possessed by the old people and into their ascertained needs before such a programme is embarked upon.

168

4 *Group psychotherapy* The basic idea behind the use of psychotherapy with the aged is that older people have a considerable amount of knowledge in the form of experience. If this knowledge and sensitivity can be used, they can become constructive participants in their environment instead of passive bystanders. The methods used are the same as group psychotherapy with any other group of clients, the ventilation of problems, the enhancement of self, and awareness of the responses of others.

The therapy was aimed at increasing the social functioning of the elderly despite the handicaps of chronic physical symptoms. Some improvement along these lines has been recorded, but it is generally felt that such groups would not succeed if they attempted to avoid conflict, controversy, and confrontation.

Groups in health care

Very little emphasis seems to have been placed on the use of groups in this field. Traditionally and practically dominated by the medical profession, psychotherapy to combat the emotional problems of illness looms large. In most instances work is centred round groups of people with the same sort of problem on the assumption that by contact and communication the experience of sharing knowledge, feelings, and responses will enhance both the emotional adjustment of most and also their practical ability to cope.

The whole gamut of groups is used here from social and leisure activities to group psychotherapy. Activities range equally widely but there seems to be a preference for discussion groups. Some of the aims which are offered are as follows:

1 Socialization and involvement in the community.
2 To define problem areas and to explore potential.
3 To change attitudes and behaviour.
4 To enhance the developmental process.
5 To increase awareness.
6 To reduce over dependence.

Among the clientele of such groups have been: adolescents with problems ranging through shyness, skin diseases, brain damage, learning problems, physical handicap, etc. Adults also have figured in such groups as parents of children with particular problems, or those with difficulties of their own.

Many problems have been listed as being dealt with in groups. Deaf children were noted as having problems in the area of language skills and demonstrated maturational lags and lack of experiences common to hearing children of the same age. Environmental problems are also common. Isolation has become a major factor in the lives of the handicapped. The organizational structure in which these groups were formed frequently created problems of non-attendance, hostility from other staff members, and lack of understanding.

Most of these groups take place within a hospital setting though schools and community centres, homes, and out-patient clinics have also been used.

Some of the special techniques used are of interest. One group worker referred to the use of informal groups by which he meant accepting groups which collected in the corner of the ward. With deaf children it has been found that there is a great need for the group leader to be able to 'concretize' abstract concepts clearly, to use constant repetition, and to insist on the memorizing of a few basic ground rules. Handicapped people seem to have been integrated into already existing groups in community centres and great use seems to have been made of co-leaders of different sex.

There is a strong note of optimism in the reports of these groups. Emphasis is placed upon the fact that learning took place, maladaptive patterns of behaviour were interrupted, and improvements in making relationships and in the ability to communicate were noted.

Obviously there are wide areas in this field in which group approaches have not been tried or at least the attempts have not been recorded. It is clear that where people have to face a considerable change in life style, the possibility of sharing this traumatic experience with others in a similar situation can be very beneficial. Whatever slant the group leader may take, the shared experience should include social, learning, and personal growth factors to be most effective. Obviously leadership in these kinds of groups needs to be informed and also to be informative. Environmental and organizational constraints abound and need careful consideration so that the purposes which are set for the group are possible of achievement.

It must be much more than apparent from what has been written so far that groups are ubiquitous, while not always clearly recognized for what they are, in the sense that few people ever recognize clearly what is happening under their noses as it were until experience or interest have taught them to observe clearly.

The interesting point is that wherever a collection of people exist as such over a period of time, then the group forces, which I have called processes here, operate. Another fact which also fascinates is that some people early in their lives become aware of the interaction between members of a group and become able to intervene, monitor, and direct if they so wish. A third interesting point lies in the situation which can be created when such a person does make an attempt to get the group to work more efficiently. As we have seen this is inevitably done by some process of emphasis and selection usually based upon a preconceived notion of what would be desirable under the prevailing circumstances. Thus some behaviours are created and others eliminated or modified, and direction and a degree of control given to the activities of the group.

Inter group rivalry

Probably one of the simplest shapes of 'groupness' which shows up is in the form of rivalry between different collections of people. This tends to be enhanced in childhood by friendship gangs and team games, which is one of the reasons why most people in this country at least have the basic sense that group activities are competitive and that rivalry between groups is not only to be expected but desired.

171

This essence of rivalry and competition tends to be fostered during childhood and is an inevitable consequence of the use of example and exhortation. Of course this is one of the factors that helps to generate the fear of being rejected, i.e. because one's contribution to the group effort may not be adequate. Another consequence is individualistic in that people tend to make themselves independent by being self-sufficient. So this in turn makes people increasingly suspicious of group ideas, especially where these involve some degree of surrender of personal autonomy in order to add to the public store of good.

In other words society tends to stress the competitive nature of group activity and not the co-operative. Subordination of the individual to the group ideal is achieved more for the purpose of winning against other similar groups than as an end in itself. The outcome of this can be seen in the way in which people from different groups both nationally and internationally find it hard to live in harmony with one another and are suspicious of each other's motives, unless there is some overriding factor which supersedes their individual beliefs and experiences, e.g. security, a common aggressor, a religious belief etc.

This is not to say that competition is unhealthy, but it does breed a sense of suspicion about the motives of those who belong to groups other than the one in which one's own membership reposes, especially if they exist for similar purposes. Like all human factors which become the sole purpose of existence, competition can become destructive or wasteful of other aspects of personality.

In families, schools, places of work, leisure activities, and all kinds of other human organizations, groups are constructed to achieve purposes which individuals either cannot at all or readily achieve by themselves. Loyalties develop and change and occasionally events occur which demonstrate how powerful are the group influences at work. The purpose of this part of the book has been to show what can happen when some understanding of group processes is applied to those problems which surround us. Most human relationships are of the nature of being group occurrences and it is here that the spin-off has great benefit. Not only is it possible to apply knowledge to actual created groups for beneficial outcomes, but also there is the distinct possibility that we will understand better the general pressures to which we are subjected every moment of our existence. Such knowledge may free us to make choices rather than be moved by forces which not only do we not appreciate but do not even know exist.

10 Knowledge and skill do not grow on trees

> If knowledge gets far ahead of being, it becomes theoretical and abstract and inapplicable to life, or actually harmful, because instead of serving life and helping people the better to struggle with the difficulties they meet, it begins to complicate man's life, brings new difficulties into it, new troubles and calamities which were not there before. [1]

> There is no convincing evidence to show that teaching a pupil *about* language does anything to improve his performance in it. On the other hand, there is abundant evidence to show that constant practice in talking and writing, especially where the pupil's experience, interest and imagination are involved, significantly improve performance. [2]

By using these two quotations from very different sources I hope to show that knowledge has to be useful and adapted to the needs of those who work with it, at least as far as professional knowledge is concerned. Second, I hope that the remarks quoted will help to indicate that where a particular skill is required, then talking *about* it is of little practical value in increasing the ability to perform.

In the Wilson quotation if one substitutes 'learner' for 'pupil' and 'groupwork' for 'language', the analogy is more or less complete. Both are practical skills, both require creative practice. Groupwork may be considered to be a more complex piece of social behaviour than speaking a language; there is the danger that it will therefore be subjected to much more teaching *about*.

Group workers, like everyone else, need to learn their trade,

1   P. D. Ouspensky, *In Search of the Miraculous* (London, Routledge and Kegan Paul, 1950), p.65.
2   R. Wilson, in *The Critical Survey*, vol.5, no.3, winter 1971, p.221.

and without any doubt the best way of doing this is in a kind of apprenticeship situation. No one every truly learned how to operate in a group situation from reading a book, no matter how good or how well written. Therefore all potential group workers have to face the situation that they will have to undergo some form of supervised experience with an experienced group worker who, if they are fortunate, will also be an experienced teacher.

The purpose of this chapter is to try and give some simple guide lines to the learning process which can get very complicated, especially when it is realized that the main way of teaching people about groups is to expect them to analyse the dynamics of a group of which they are members. To put it another way the learner has to develop a kind of schizophrenic approach, being able to be an active and participating member of his group and at the same time an impartial observer of the forces which are affecting him and all the other members. It is not surprising that most people find this daunting if not impossible. However as the ability to function as a group member as well as be the observer is absolutely essential to being a good group leader there is no other satisfactory way around this problem.

As we have seen there are a great many different kinds of groups run by people with very different theoretical understandings of the human condition. But basically all groups have the same fundamental properties which we have called their processes. The difference in the groups lies in which of the processes the group leader chooses to emphasize and which to ignore, which of the styles of leadership is most compatible with his theoretical orientation and which is not.

Thus the first problem a beginner faces is whether to commit himself to one kind of group approach or another. The choice of mentor will in fact mean that this choice has been made, for the style of the teacher will have a lasting effect upon the student. This problem is not so simple as it would appear, because it is also complicated by the fact that a large number of practitioners have got an individualist approach to working with groups, i.e. they are prepared to work only with the individual in a group situation.

However before starting to look at the kind of group which might be available for the learner it is necessary to make a passing reference to the learning problems themselves.

The first of these is an attitude of mind which tends to prevail with regard to what might be loosely called 'social skills'. By this I mean all those areas of understanding of, and working with, people. So many people believe that because they have achieved whatever age they have without major catastrophe that they are therefore 'by the light of nature' experts in human relationships. This 'natural' approach to learning about human behaviour makes life for the teacher very complicated. Why? Well if everyone actually learns all their coping skills in a natural way, then any teaching about them is immediately seen as artificial and 'unnatural' and in this way resisted.

The first point that has to be got over then is that the social skills which are acquired 'naturally' are at best what could be called 'parochial', that is they refer to, and are adequate for, only the limited situations in which they grew. This is true in most cases, but not for people whose life experience has been very wide and diffuse. They may, but only may, have been compelled by circumstances to learn so much more because of the number of situations which they have had to face.

The argument can be continued along the lines that if the natural processes of learning social skills are so effective why have we got so many problems of human relationships? The answer can only lie in the fact that the so called 'natural' learning is only adequate for limited situations.

It is essential that this point be understood because what really requires a very serious study to be effective will only receive cursory attention if it is not. So we can say that in order to learn about group behaviour a great deal of hard work is necessary and a willingness to learn and to acquire skills in social relationships. There is so much which is known about the ways in which human beings behave and hardly any of it is consciously used to improve the lot of people except by a very few. Of course to make this adjustment in attitude requires some encouragement because our society regards learning about human behaviour as something which is akin to witchcraft or at least to an unwarranted interference in the lives of others.

Culturally we are conditioned to accept our social training as being adequate and this leads us directly into the second area of possible learning difficulty.

Effective groupwork is concerned above everything else with observation. If a group leader or member is not able to see what is going on under his very nose, then in no way can he be expected to do anything about it. It is always a precondition of action that the person who makes it is aware that some kind of action is necessary. He may of course be wrong, but at least he has a perception of the situation which indicates the desirability of some form of action. Without this perception nothing will be done.

Our society does not approve of staring. It embarrasses people and is generally taken as being rude. But if we are to be able to see what people are doing, then there is no substitute for staring and for staring hard. It is a truism of life that there is a great deal of difference between looking and seeing. For most of our daily lives we look at things but we rarely see them in the sense that if we are asked to describe them later we have only the vaguest knowledge of what was there. Of course this monitoring of what we pay attention to helps us to concentrate on the things which are of immediate importance and to screen out those myriads of impressions which would only confuse the issue and which are not seen as being either dangerous or relevant in some other way. If we were to try to pay equal attention to all the impressions which our senses offer us, we would I think soon become incapable of any form of existence.

So when we say that the first requisite of learning about groups is to watch what groups do, we are faced with the possible inhibition which society imposes on such an activity. Any programme designed to make people aware of group processes has therefore to build in some form of exercise which will free people from this embarrassment.

The third learning difficulty is concerned with the fact that understanding of group processes is usually obtained by experiencing at first hand what those processes can do. In other words one has to feel what they do by being the object upon which the processes are working. Thus it is of little practical value to know that groups apply pressure to their members to conform, if one has not felt what such pressure is actually like.

Thus to recapitulate the three major learning problems:

1 The resistance to the idea that social skills can be, or need to be, learned.
2 The resistance to the idea that observation of others is an essential part of learning about behaviour because of the inbuilt sense of embarrassment.
3 The need to recognize that experience of what the quality of group pressure is like has to be personal, so that some idea of its possible effects on others can be gained.

Of course almost any group will do as a source of interaction which can be observed, but, as I hope to show, special exercises and involvement are necessary to be able to understand the other factors involved.

Given that the necessity of learning about human behaviour has been accepted, then the first point which has to be made is to recognize the way in which a group is effective in influencing the behaviour of its members. This can be done by a fairly careful analysis of any group of which one is a member, say a family or a friendship group, but it must be one in which the basic requirement for influence is fulfilled, i.e. that we have a reasonably strong desire to be accepted as a member of the group. Remember the law goes: *The greater the need the individual member has of being accepted by the group, the greater the pressure the group can exert upon him provided there are no known or acceptable alternatives.*

When one starts to look at the influence groups have in this way a strange new world can emerge. Actions which we have thought to have taken upon our own initiative are now seen to be caused by the effects we anticipate they would have upon the group. The network of influence is seen to spread very wide indeed and to cover a great part of our lives. Let us take just

178

one very illuminating example, the way in which decisions are made in a group.

Very often people can be heard to say that a group made some decision or other. Now I would maintain that this is incorrect in that no group ever made any decision. What usually happens is that the group as a whole agrees to accept some point put forward by an individual. This implies that the group ratifies what one of its members has suggested. Much has to be learned about the ways in which decisions are influenced by individuals and how they are also arrived at because lack of positive disagreement is taken as consent. This being so, one can say that any member of a group who disagrees with a group decision after it has been made has only himself to blame. Unless he was the subject of a deliberate campaign to exclude him, he should have realized that his opposition to the proposal can only be effective if it is made plain. This of course applies to all other kinds of feelings that members may have and seems to be one of the hardest lessons that group members have to learn. It is no good assuming that others in the group will recognize your feelings in some telepathic way. What you feel has to be made explicit so that what is truly the opinion of the group can be arrived at.

One very simple way in which the problem of decision-making in a group can be made clear to people learning about group behaviour is to set a group of learners a task which is (a) time-limited and (b) requires the co-operation of all the members of the group to perform. If someone who is not a member of the group can be put in as a non-participating observer, so much the better. Given the time factor, which puts pressure upon the group to complete the task, then many facets of group behaviour can emerge — for instance who recognizes the limitations, who offers suggestions, how are roles allocated and who assumes leadership etc. When such a group is asked to report back on how they achieved their task one fact becomes obvious immediately and that is, because they were involved in doing something, they have only the vaguest idea how what they did was achieved. This is where the observer comes in. He can feed back to the members of the group a fairly impartial account of what he saw. When this is checked against what the members remember of their behaviour some startling contrasts appear.

Certain members are seen to have taken control of the situation and manipulated it to a given end, although this may not have been obvious to those involved at the time. They are the people who fulfilled the three necessary pre-conditions for making a leadership act:

1 Recognized that something needed to be done.
2 Felt they possessed the resources to do it.
3 Felt it was worth the risk.

Of course the task itself in this exercise is of marginal importance but it does help if it can be something which the participants see as being useful or amusing. I frequently use the idea of the group casting themselves in a small drama about some well-defined theme or ask them to compile a list of group members in order of worthiness, each member to argue for his inclusion in the list at a given point etc. Games they may be, but these exercises begin to develop skills which are essential to the use and understanding of group behaviour.

Take for example the act of decision-making at which we have just been looking. It is essential that any group leader should be able to recognize the process when it occurs; he should also be able to see which members are affecting the process and in what direction and to what extent. Given that he can do this, then he has to decide whether he will intervene in the process, at what level and with what effect.

Films of group actions and video tapes are very useful here because the action of the group can be played over and over again in order to show exactly what happened. Indeed audio tapes can be used just as well wherever a one-way screen is available, and is another way of watching what goes on, though this possesses the defects of not being able to provide playback and to be susceptible to objection on ethical grounds. The last point is bound up with what was mentioned earlier in connection with society's view about watching people. It is especially highlighted here if the group being watched are unaware of the fact.

Video tape has been widely introduced as a very useful medium in learning about group behaviour. For me it has one or two handicaps which reduce its actual value very considerably. However well equipped the studio, there is no way that I have been able to discover which actually allows the recorder to cover the total interaction of the group without being so far away that the resulting film is pointless for learning purposes. Most groups sit in a circle which has many practical values as was explained earlier. It is inevitable that some members will have their backs to the camera. If one tries to overcome this by using several cameras, then the problem of selection, which shot to record out of those which are available, emerges as crucial. Just take the fact that it is customary in our society that when one person in a group is speaking for the others to look at him. Apart from any other significance that this act may have, it puts each member in touch with all the non-verbal cues which the speaker is giving which as we know may be a very substantial part of his message, especially if it is concerned with feelings. But a group leader has a need to know not only what the speaker is doing but how every other member of the group is responding to what he is doing. It is not possible to record both these needs upon one tape. Even split screen does not give the required information. It boils down to the fact that any recording of a group is bound to be both selective and unrepresentative of the complex interaction patterns which even a very simple group provides.

Of course video tapes are valuable, even knowing that they give a selective and distorted picture of what was available. For instance they are very effective in showing group members roughly how they are perceived by other members in the group. Now there appears to be a very small time when someone sees himself on the screen for the first time in which there is the possibility of learning quite a lot about one's image. Then it seems as though the mind intervenes in some way and the perception of the image is readjusted to suit what was expected, and the possibility of learning something about an outsider's viewpoint of ourselves disappears and does not reoccur with anything like the same impact thereafter.

Tape recordings can be used to help group members analyse the group process in wide sweeps rather than in terms of immediate interaction. What the group is doing as opposed to what individual members are saying sometimes emerges very clearly from a recording. Of course all the non-verbal cues, apart from tone of voice, are missing and the exercise is time-consuming in that each tape takes as long to listen to as it did to record in the first instance.

However such tapes are very useful in showing the style of people's contribution to the group, the timing and frequency of interventions, and so on.

Exercises in designing groups can be created from actual situations. For instance a problem can be set along the lines of 'This is the environment; these are the possible candidates; this is a rough analysis of the problems, difficulties or whatever that it is proposed to deal with; these are the resources and facilities available … now design a group which will best meet the needs which you can see.' This is an academic exercise, but at least it encourages people to see the conceptualization stage of group-work as being of vital importance and tends to teach people how to avoid the very common pitfalls which we have looked at earlier.

There is no real substitute for actually operating in a group with a leader whose purpose is to instruct. As things happen within the group such a leader is going to ask 'What do you see, feel is happening now?' Thus constantly dragging members back to the prime purpose of the group when they are likely to have become involved in participation. This has obvious difficulties of course. Every time that the leader draws members' awareness to the process of the group, he is in danger of disturbing the flow of that process and of introducing a strong sense of artificiality into the proceedings. However, as the group proceeds and other members take up the idea of examining what is going on, then the purpose of the group switches to learning by self-examination and the sense of artificiality tends to disappear and a whole series of enquiring and valuable habits have started to become established in the members.

Of course whenever a group is started by someone without much experience as part of their learning schedule, then it is advisable to have another person available to act as consultant, someone who can provide the necessary cover and experience so that the tyro can check what he is doing, feeling, seeing against a more mature judgement.

As has been said earlier about recording groups, the only real way in which one can realize what is happening is to keep a diary. This should be written up as soon after the group has ceased each session as is possible. Over time, patterns of events will emerge, the effectiveness of decisions taken and interventions made will show in ways that they never would close to the time when they occurred. The pressure of events outside the group is sufficient to obliterate or distort what one remembers about particular sessions if there is no kind of recorded data to which reference can be made.

If a group is being run with a co-leader, then obviously one leader can be responsible for recording while the other is concerned with the actual leadership of the group. If these roles are taken in turn then valuable experience of being in the group and of watching the large moves which are being made can be obtained. Co-leaders are also very useful in sharing the load and as a check upon each other's behaviour particularly in areas which may have remained blind otherwise.

A training programme designed to help people understand how groups operate is very difficult to plan effectively. It must start from what the people involved already know about groups and also from what they have thought and felt about groups. For instance there is so much written about certain kinds of groups these days that it would be very unusual indeed if some member of a collection of students of groupwork had not had some experience of, say, a sensitivity training group, or at least of some form of personal-growth group.

Now these experiences will condition the approach a person makes to any new group experience and will certainly influence both the nature of the learning and the selection of it. Many people expect all group training to be of the personal-growth kind, some are so defended that it proves almost impossible for them to learn anything. It is necessary to understand that factors like these are involved and that learning to be a group worker is not the same as studying economics, because there is a direct involvement of the person both in the learning and in the execution.

If at all possible the feelings that people have about groups should be brought out into the open where they can be discussed and their influence upon the ability of the learner to learn discounted. In itself the process of clearing expectations and hidden feelings like this is a good example of the way in which a group will operate. Clearly if the process is well done, then each member of the group will have both a better chance to learn and will also have a sense that this was achieved in co-operation with the other members of the group. The whole basis of group success — shared experience — has already started to operate.

A most effective method of teaching in the group situation is by example. If the leader is a good one, then his group members will tend to emulate his methods. The leader can thus consciously influence the way in which his members will go by displaying the behaviour patterns which he feels they could emulate with benefit. He establishes his own behaviour as a role model, as we have seen earlier. This is not just a technique in the learning situation but also a very effective act of leadership in an actual group.

Interestingly enough this ties in very closely with the idea that behaviour patterns are much more likely to be accepted by others as true than the spoken word. Whatever a group leader says he is doing it is what he actually does which will turn out to be the important factor. If he says it is necessary to be sensitive and then behaves in an insensitive way, the learning for his members is remarkably clear — either he is a bad leader or he does not believe what he is saying or worst of all he cares so little about the present group membership that he is not concerned about the discrepancy in the two areas of his behaviour. If he shows that he is not able to accept feedback about his leadership behaviour from his group, then it is not likely that his dictum that feedback is an important part of understanding group behaviour will gain much credence with them.

This is a very important part of the learning situation which many people find very hard to accept. All that we know about non-verbal communication would tend to confirm that where anxiety and strangeness combine to make people feel that they are not as secure as they would like to be, i.e. in a new learning situation where people are exposed to new ideas and the scrutiny of others, then they become particularly sensitive to the behaviour of others who are important, and in particular to all the non-verbal communications.

Of course anyone learning about groups needs to be able to practise what he has learnt. There is therefore great need to give people the opportunity to take over groups and to try to exercise leadership, to try to guide groups; to try to adapt their behaviour to the perceived needs of the group and to get feedback about the way in which the group members felt they were being handled. It is essential that trainees should practise different styles of leadership no matter how much they feel that one particular style is adapted to their personality. It is not always possible or even desirable that a group leader should have one style; he should be free to adapt his approach to what he can see is going to meet the group's needs most effectively. All leaders should have the chance to be directive, for the beginning of any group places great demands for security and certainty upon the leader and some approaches demand this kind of certainty all the way through.

Roleplay sessions and simulated situations are excellent for providing a kind of dummy run for those who want to feel what it is like to be in the leader's position before they actually have to play in a serious situation and have to become involved with others who may well be very dependent upon them.

Books and other written material are the sources of ideas and approaches; of records of the ways in which other people have tackled similar problems, and of the theory which is available about groups and groupwork. The translation of ideas into practice requires different skills from those required to produce the ideas, and frequently ideas have to be modified in practice to fit the situations in which they are being used.

In my experience information is fairly useless unless it is directly related to need. Thus when the answer to my question 'How are you going to cope with this?' or 'What are you going to do next?' produces the answer 'I don't know' or 'I am not sure', then information which is relevant to the situation can be advanced in the knowledge that the need for it has been seen and that its immediate value will also be seen, and finally that its use there and then will ensure that this particular piece of information will become the property of the user. A fundamental learning rule will have been adhered to, that in learning complex skills information is only useful in so far as it becomes the property of the person who wishes to use it.

Learning about groups is a special form of learning in that the groups which are formed to do the learning are able to study their own behaviour in the knowledge that it represents a fairly accurate picture of what goes on in other groups. The emphasis will be different but very little else. Of course this fact can obscure what is going on for some people whose ideas of learning cannot readily be adapted to this kind of approach because they see that all groups are different and pursue different purposes or because self examination does not come easily to them.

When the subject of one's study is people and their behaviour, then one is surrounded by one's subject matter and in fact is part of it. There is no shortage of material; all that is needed is a little expert guidance as to what is of prime importance to start with.

A final word

... the point is that a 'group' is the beginning of everything.
One man can do nothing, can attain nothing. A group with a
real leader can do more. A group of people can do what one
man can never do.[3]

I have attempted to set down as clearly as possible and enu-
merate the different 'ways' in which the principal groupwork
tasks may be essayed. It has always seemed to me that this was
one of the areas of greatest confusion for those interested in
working with groups, i.e. that there was little or no indication of
the choices which are available in the literature on the subject.
Either one adhered to the dogma of a particular kind of group
backed by a particular theory of behaviour and a pragmatic
collection of practice principles or one followed the precepts of a
particular profession's use of groups, i.e. psychiatry, social work,
education etc. This has led inevitably to some inappropriate use
of groups on the grounds that to do what was obviously needed
in the particular circumstances did not conform to the apparent
dogma of a particular form of 'groupwork' and could not
therefore be 'correct'.

For example most textbooks on groupwork lay particular
emphasis upon the need for careful selection of people to form a
group, ignoring the fact that many people working with groups
are faced with either an inadequate number of people to select
from, or that any kind of selection may be invidious not to say
damaging. The recognition that the classic form of selection is
only one form of several can be very reassuring to those group
practitioners who find themselves in this kind of situation. They
recognize that while the 'funnel' ensures certain characteristics
in a group and eliminates others, the use of different forms of
selection right up to and including non-selection ensures the
presence of different characteristics and the elimination of still
others. The skill lies in being able to recognize what remains and

3 P.D. Ouspensky, *In Search of the Miraculous* (London, Routledge and Kegan
   Paul, 1950), p.30.

what goes out and whether what is left is compatible with what is needed in order for the group to be effective in its chosen role.

I have tried to show that groupwork is an active and interventionist skill. Even the way to learn about groups has to be an active one. I suspect that over the years I have convinced myself that some people have a greater ability to become group workers than others, though I am not able to offer any real evidence of this. However, I have noticed that some people seem much happier than others in trying to keep a number of people under their observation at one time. I suppose this may be something to do with the way in which they have been in contact with people during the process of growing-up or even the number of people that they are used to coping with in a family situation. Whatever it may be, these people seem almost instinctively to know that in a group they cannot afford to keep their gaze locked on to one person at a time. They move their heads about, keeping the whole group under constant surveillance and thus stand a much better chance of seeing what the responses of the group are to anything which happens.

I suppose that it is necessary to stress for one last time the basic fact that all groups of people behave fundamentally in the same ways. The major differences being which of these ways are emphasized because of the peculiar composition of any group and which are not. If this point is accepted, then learning about groups can become a basic operation and the processes ubiquitous. Whatever slant one then develops towards the understanding of human behaviour can be applied in the use one makes of the basic group processes either in terms of selection, interpretation or intervention.

Finally there is no substitute for integrated and ordered experience, but be careful where and with whom you attempt to obtain it. There is no register of practitioners in this country and anyone can say he is an expert in groupwork without needing to produce any evidence to prove the point. All the factors which groups produce which are beneficial can also be destructive when handled carelessly or with deliberate intent to harm. It is a recognized fact that as we advance our knowledge about human

188

behaviour that knowledge can be used in a variety of ways. The knowledge itself is neutral; the uses to which it can be put may range from beneficial through to destructive.

No man is born unto himself alone,
Who lives unto himself, he lives to none.

Francis Quarles, 1592 - 1644,
Esther Sec 1, Medit.1.

Reading list

This list has been kept very short. The basic criteria for the inclusion of any title are that it is useful, simple, and easily obtainable.

W.J.H. Sprott (1958) *Human Groups*. Harmondsworth: Penguin.
Judy Gahagan (1975) *Interpersonal and Group Behaviour*. London: Methuen.
A. Blumberg and R.T. Golembiewski (1976) *Learning and Change in Groups*. Harmondsworth: Penguin.
L. Button (1974) *Developmental Groupwork with Adolescents*. University of London Press Ltd.
B. Davies (1975) *The Use of Groups in Social Work Practice*. London: Routledge and Kegan Paul.
T. Douglas (1976) *Groupwork Practice*. London: Tavistock.
Sue Jennings (1973) *Remedial Drama*. London: Pitman Publishing.

190

F. Milson (1973) *An Introduction to Groupwork Skill*. London: Routledge and Kegan Paul.

C. Rogers (1969) *Encounter Groups*. Harmondsworth: Penguin.

H. Walton (ed.) (1971) *Small Group Psychotherapy*. Harmondsworth: Penguin.

For further reading, reference should be made to the extensive bibliographies in some of the books listed above, and to the professional journals in social work, psychology, psychiatry, sociology, and in education.

Index

formed groups, 40, 43, 56-7
'funnel', the, 84-6, 187

games, 94, 180
Gendlin, E.T., 96
Gestalt psychology, 31
'Gingerbread Group', 25-6
goal achievement, 143
goal formation, 45, 46, 50-1
Golembiewski, R., 37n.
Greenwood, N., 109
ground rules, 95-9
group counselling, 167-8
group development, 37-41, 46, 49
group discussion, 167-8
'group living', 160
group pressure, 4-5, 45, 53, 178
group processes, 12, 43
group psychotherapy, 169
groups
    beginnings of, 1-2
    classification of, 29-32
    as context and instrument, 32-4
    creation of, 99-101
    design of, 64-9, 182
    maintenance of, 115, 119
    mechanics of, 90
    operation of, 118-20
    origins of, 21-9
    a philosophy of, 148-52
    running, xii, 102
    setting up, 62-4
    size of, 58-9
    sources of power of, 5-6
    stagnation of, 38, 93
    starting, 82-3
    termination of, 142-3, 153-5
groups, examples of
    child minders, 113, 145
    church members, 130-1
    city children, 83-4
    elderly men, 117-18
    family, 23-4
    foster parents, 136
    probationers, 54
    probation officers, 83
    psychiatric patients, 90, 103-4,
        114-15, 146-7

groups, examples of, *cont.*,
    social work students, 13-18, 85-6,
        99-101, 118-20, 139-41, 184
    women prisoners, 128
groupwork literature, 20, 37, 52
groupwork, training for, 174-5
Guyon, D., 156n.

health care, groups in, 169-71
Heap, K., 117 *and* n.
hiding, 59, 108
Hodge, J., 81n.

individual, the, ix-x, 148-9
influence, 46, 52-3, 178
information
    and contract, 100
    related to need, 186
    shared, 92
    ways of absorbing, 98-9
    ways of passing on, 29-30
initiation ceremonies, 114-15
input, 79, 101, 119
instrument, 32-4
interaction, 3, 44-8
inter group rivalry, 171-3
interpretation, 51
intervention, 44, 124-7
    appropriate, 112-4
    examples of, 139-41
    and leadership, 124-7
interviews, 103
introductions, 68
isolates, 65, 73
isolation, fears, of, 2-3, 5, 43

Jennings, S., 158-8 *and* n.
judgement, 144

knowledge
    and group design, 65
    of group members, 77
    specialist, 10-11
    superior, 75, 151
    use of, 174